Endorsements

I absolutely encourage the reading of *Disrupting Whiteness,* chiefly as a primer for those who don't have the benefit of historical reflection but also for those who perpetuate historical racial oppression. Reading it can create an opening for self-correction and redemption. This is an important and value-added read.

—Malcolm Byrd
CEO of Forum Philly and President of NewCORE

Written in accessible language, through a spirit of humility, dialogue and a fostering of racial harmony, this book especially invites white people to peer in the mirror in order to take the first step to authentically encounter head on what Richard Wright calls a white problem.

—James D. Kirylo
Professor of Education
University of South Carolina

Drick Boyd offers a practical and transformative process for white people to do their own work on racism. If you are white, buy this book. If you are Black, Indigenous, a Person of Color, buy this book for your white friends. The future of white people in the United States depends on their joining the larger conversation on racism.

—Curtiss Paul DeYoung
CEO, Minnesota Council of Churches

A practical, accessible and engaging read that invites principled action and thoughtful participation in the work of dismantling racism. Drick offers the best of research and grassroots experience with a proven process to deepen conversations about racism. A gem.

—Dr. Tobin Miller Shearer
Associate Professor of History and Director of
African American Studies at the University of Montana
Author: Enter the River: Healing Steps from White
Privilege Toward Racial Reconciliation

In *Disrupting Whiteness*, Boyd aptly hones in on the thinking and feeling behind white paralysis, shame and silence around race/racism, and offers strategies for moving from denial and discussion-dodging to honest transformation. The power of listening to and revisiting our own stories about becoming racialized can begin a process of healing. Boyd joins a current overdue collection of white writers and activists who not only highlight the ways racism hurts and limits the lives of BIPOC people, but who look squarely at the ways racism and white supremacy cripples and dehumanizes white people. Others have observed that something must be lacking in white humanity, or what DiAngelo calls "white fragility" and it requires that white people do their work for their own salvation. *Disrupting Whiteness* is important and necessary reading for white people and BIPOC alike. Thank you, Drick, for your story, commitment and friendship.

—Calenthia S. Dowdy, Ph.D.
facilitator/consultant with Roots of Justice, Inc.

There were days when I dreamed of this book. There were seasons when I knew that a book like this was needed. I knew that in the work of creating community across the barriers of race and ethnicities, there needed to be a book that helped white people talk to other white people about race. I didn't necessarily think it would be written, but Drick Boyd through *Disrupting Whiteness* has written that book and turned the dream into a reality. The reader is not simply reading a book but is invited to engage a process that has the potential to lead to change and transformation both in their lives and in the life of their community. This model will help people learn their own truth and, in learning that truth, they will also be enabled to hear and learn from the truth of others. This is not quick work nor is it work for the faint of heart, but it is important work. The world will be different because individuals and communities engage in the work outlined in this book.

—Rev. Dr. Marsha Brown Woodard
Palmer Theological Seminary

Disrupting Whiteness: Talking with White People About Racism is an excellent text not only for teachers and activists, but for the broader public. When it comes to social-movement organizing, there is an idea that transformative thinking begins at the direct action, but as Boyd describes, it starts inward. As Black movements grow and create change, it's important for white people to be on the front lines while reflecting on how our structure has hidden their advantages within our system. While that can be hard to do, Boyd provides a pathway for that work. A must-read!

—Dr. Christina Jackson, Ph.D.
Assistant Professor of Sociology, Stockton University
Author of Embodied Difference: Divergent Bodies in Public Discourse *and* Black In America: The Paradox of the Color Line

If you, like me, have an ounce of hope left amidst our current cultural moment of racial strife, and the faith of a mustard seed that God truly meant what he said when he taught his disciples to pray "on earth as it is in heaven," then this book is for you. Drick Boyd has been leaning hard into the work of racial justice for five decades, and has finally put forth one of the most practical and prophetic books on addressing white supremacy that's ever been written. As a former student, I can attest to his commitment to both empathetic listening and authentic dialog, which he proposes in this book as the foundational ingredients to courageously confront the sins of racism in our country. My hope is that this book sparks more than interest, but rather a movement characterized by vulnerable conversations and bold relationships that result in the healing of both the oppressed and the oppressor.

—Dustin Tommey, Executive Director
City Fields CDC, Cleveland, Tennessee

Drick Boyd's latest work is essentially an invitation—specifically, an invitation to transformative dialogue intended to "help those who are concerned about the rising tide of overt and covert racism in U.S. society to have conversations about these issues with white co-workers, friends, acquaintances and family members." Befitting the author's modus operandi exhibited in his teaching, writing and other work, this is not a book intended primarily for detached, value-neutral intellectual dissection; at its core, the book's project is to encourage self-examination as a starting point for action. It is a roadmap for engagement, a conversation starter at the grassroots level, a practical guide to and invitation for critical dialog with a most determined and consequential aim: "to transform ourselves as we also work to change the racist structures and systems in our society." With humility and prophetic earnestness, Boyd is forceful in suggesting that in dealing with what he calls the addiction to "the drug of white superiority," bystander apathy is not an option. The cumulative effect of the succession of racial atrocities and tragedies unfolding all around the country is to render imperative and anything but elective the sort of critical engagement Boyd is calling for. His methodological approach—based on storytelling, empathic listening and dialogue—is one that models and promises precisely the kind of authenticity and urgency of engagement that is often difficult to achieve in the context of entrenched patterns of racial privilege and hegemony, but that likely holds the key to attaining the transformative understanding and real change we as a society so desperately need.

—Dr. Joao Monteiro
Professor of Sociology, Eastern University

Drick Boyd's *Disrupting Whiteness: Talking with White People About Racism* is an excellent book addressing how to talk to white people to understand and do something about racism. Boyd makes a disturbing assumption that "no white person in the U.S. context can contend that he or she is free of racism." All whites are racist. Some, like Boyd himself, are recovering racists—ones who acknowledge that whites have social, economic, political and racial advantages over minority racial groups, what Boyd terms the Black, Indigenous and People of Color (BIPOC). Boyd's goal is to get whites to be recovering racists who confront the racism scourge. He argues that addressing the racism scourge for whites demands knowing their race history as well as that of the BIPOC, then engaging in transformative dialogue. The goal is to enable the whites to realize that racism is destructive not only to the BIPOC but to them as well, and to engage them in seeking ways of addressing it. I enjoyed and learned a lot from reading this book.

—Dr. Mike Mtika
Professor of Sociology, Eastern University

DISRUPTING WHITENESS

TALKING WITH WHITE PEOPLE ABOUT RACISM

DRICK BOYD

Copyright © 2021 Drick Boyd

All rights reserved, including the right to reproduce this book or portions thereof
in any form whatsoever. For information on reproducing or licensing rights,
please contact Arch Street Press: contact@archstreetpress.org.

First Arch Street Press edition: January 2021

ARCH STREET PRESS, ARCH ST. PRESS
and colophon are registered trademarks of Arch Street Press.

For information about special discounts for bulk and nonprofit purchases,
please contact Arch Street Press: sales@archstreetpress.org.

Book design by idesign communications
Cover design by idesign communications

Library of Congress Cataloging-in-Publication Data is available.

ISBN: 978-1-938798-38-2 (paperback)
ISBN: 978-1-938798-37-5 (e-book)

Contents

Preface

What happens to a dream deferred?

Does it dry up
like a raisin in the sun?
Or fester like a sore—
And then run?
Does it stink like rotten meat?
Or crust and sugar over—
Like a syrupy sweet.

Maybe it just sags
Like a heavy load.

Or does it explode?

—Langston Hughes

A Moment, a Movement or a Revolution?

As I write these words, our nation is in the midst of dramatic change, or so many hope. The dream of racial justice has too long been deferred and has exploded.

In the early months of 2020, the deadly virus originating in Wuhan, China, began spreading across the globe. By mid-March in the U.S., schools, businesses, government offices and community gatherings began being canceled or closed. Hospital emergency rooms across the country were overrun by people with the strange deadly disease referred to as COVID-19 or simply the coronavirus. New terms like "essential workers" and "social distancing" entered the American lexicon and comparisons were made to the 1918 flu epidemic that killed 50 million people worldwide and 650,000 in the United States.[1]

Over recent months, it has become clear that COVID-19 does not afflict racial and ethnic groups at the same rates. Blacks and Latinx persons, especially those with limited incomes, are infected at higher rates than whites. Reasons given include less access to healthcare, more crowded housing conditions and a higher percentage of Black and Brown persons in service-related jobs.[2]

Playing on the origins of the virus, President Trump has publicly referred to it in terms such as "the Chinese virus" and "Kung flu," inciting racist attacks on Asian Americans and their businesses.[3] According to the Asian Pacific Policy and Planning Council, "More than 2,100 anti-Asian American hate incidents related to COVID-19 were reported across the country over a three-month time span between March and June [2020]."[4]

On Monday, May 25, 2020, Minneapolis police officer Derek Chauvin pushed his knee onto the neck of George Floyd for eight minutes and 46 seconds as bystanders pleaded for him to stop. Floyd repeatedly cried out that he could not breathe. Three additional officers stood by, two holding down his feet and the third watching. A young woman videotaped the incident and in moments it went viral. An ambulance arrived, Chauvin stood up and the motionless Floyd was rushed to the hospital. An hour later, the medical examiner pronounced him dead. Two autopsies determined that he had died of asphyxiation.[5]

Beginning in Minneapolis, protests erupted all over the country in response to Floyd's unjust and unnecessary death; another Black man in a long line of Black deaths had died at the hands of police. In cities and towns across the country, crowds of all races and ages gathered, shouting "Black Lives Matter" and risking infection from the coronavirus to make their concerns known. Police in riot gear wielded clubs, sprayed tear gas and drove tanks against the mostly peaceful demonstrators.

As these events continue, there is growing urgency for significant social and structural change. Floyd's death brought heightened attention to anti-Black racism and police brutality, and led to calls for defunding the police. At the same time, protestors' demands for change have broadened to include concerns about healthcare, homelessness, LGBTQ rights and education. Those on the front lines claim they are committed to demonstrating until substantive changes in national priorities have been achieved. Time will tell if we are living in a moment, a movement or a revolution of values and priorities as a nation.

Black Lives Matter

At the forefront of the ongoing protests is the Black Lives Matter Movement. Founded by three African American women as a hashtag after the acquittal of Trayvon Martin's killer George Zimmerman in 2013, it became a national movement after the police shooting of Ferguson's Michael Brown in 2014.[6] Black Lives Matter and related organizations have captured the collective outrage over Black deaths by police all over the country and have emboldened protestors, both Black and white, to express a range of emotions—grief, anger, rage, terror and exasperation—in signs, chants and acts of civil disobedience. While these actions are directed at current atrocities, they also call to mind centuries of Black oppression and death at the hands of slaveholders, lynch mobs, segregationists and police enforcers of racist policies and practices.[7]

Author and poet Audre Lorde says anger is "a legitimate response to racial injustice and can become a powerful source of energy serving progress and change."[8] Anger has a way of bringing people together, focusing their energy on a common cause in an intense manner. The current anger has challenged the accepted norms and practices of a society that does not treat Black and Brown deaths with the same weight and significance as white deaths. That anger has gone public by taking to the streets and announcing that business as usual cannot continue as long as this pattern of death and injustice persists.

The White Response

In numbers like never before, white people—young adults, seniors and children—have joined in this call for substantive change. Companies and political leaders have publicly affirmed that Black lives do in fact matter, and statues reminiscent of the nation's racist history have been torn down or removed.

On the other hand, a significant percentage of whites have remained either silent or resistant to this recent turn of events. On social media, in counter-protests and at public forums, whites have expressed a range of responses critical of the demonstrations. Focusing on the violence that occurred in some places, these whites have expressed fear and anger at the apparent disregard for the property of storeowners. Still others have regarded the protests as a threat to the American way of life. They have demonstrated little understanding of—or empathy for—the reasons behind the rage and frustration felt by so many African Americans, and instead regard Black Lives Matter as a terrorist group.[9] In August 2020, clashes between protestors and angry white counter-protestors have led to deaths in Portland, Oregon, and Kenosha, Wisconsin,[10] a foreboding that more violent clashes might be coming. Ironically, many of these folks criticizing the current protests say they revere the late Dr. Martin Luther King, Jr., yet they forget that the same kind of criticisms were made about him when he was organizing marches and sit-ins during the Civil Rights Movement.

Disrupting Whiteness

I began writing *Disrupting Whiteness* in the aftermath of the tragic events in Charlottesville, Virginia, in August 2017. The manuscript was completed just a few weeks before George Floyd's murder. While the time, place and circumstances were different, the forces that created the racial disparities made evident during the pandemic and killed him are the same forces at work in Charlottesville, part of an historic pattern of white supremacist violence against Black and Brown people in this country. Charlottesville evoked a strong response across the nation, but it has been dwarfed by the explosion of rage, grief, trauma and anguish that erupted after Floyd's death.

This eruption makes the need to disrupt whiteness all the more urgent. There is clarity and urgency among many citizens about the injustices that have too long oppressed and dehumanized the nation's citizens of color. While changing laws and policies—and reforming institutional structures—are important, white people also need to grapple with the ways that racism has shaped their lives and the institutions of U.S.

society. This book seeks to address that need and equip readers to have meaningful and sustained conversations with white people so as to help them move from fear and disdain to understanding and support for significant societal change.

Comments on Language and Presentation

The events of summer 2020 have also caused many, including me, to re-examine the way we talk about race in America. To that end, I have chosen to use the anagram BIPOC in place of the previously standard "people of color" when referring to the nonwhite segment of the U.S. population. This designation has been widely used in this period's demonstrations and rallies. BIPOC was first brought to my attention by Layla F. Saad, the author of *White Supremacy and Me*,[11] and stands for Black, Indigenous and People of Color, acknowledging the diversity of nonwhite peoples in U.S. society and their unique struggles against racism and white supremacy.

Within literary and media circles, the issue of when and how to capitalize the names of racial and ethnic groups has been much in debate. After much consideration, I have chosen to follow the guidelines set forth by the *Columbia Journalism Review* that states: "For many people *Black* reflects a shared sense of identity and community. White carries a different set of meanings; capitalizing the word in this context risks following the lead of white supremacists."[12] Thus, I have chosen to capitalize terms like Black, Brown and Native American, while not capitalizing white. While this choice may seem grammatically inconsistent, it feels appropriate in this historical moment. When quoting authors who follow different guidelines, I have maintained their words as originally written.

Where possible, I have inserted references to events following George Floyd's death in the text. However, in seeking to do so, I soon realized that every day of the past several months brings more examples that could be included in the text and so, generally speaking, I have opted to let the insights from my pre-George Floyd reflections shine a light on the ongoing attitudes, struggles and needs to be addressed.

Acknowledgements

I want to thank all the people whose support and input have made this book possible, starting with my colleagues Tobin Miller Shearer, James Kirylo and David Tatgenhorst, who gave me substantive feedback, and my brother Winton Boyd, who encouraged and challenged me to keep the text relevant to the everyday person and not just academics; I hope I have succeeded in that. I am thankful for the members of NewCORE, whose approach to conversations on race I have adapted in this book, and am grateful to the staff at Arch Street Press—David Castro, Ann Black and Robert Rimm—whose enthusiasm for the book continues to be encouraging. I am especially indebted to Robert, who went through the manuscript page by page with me to assure that I was conveying my message as clearly as possible. I am also appreciative of all my friends, colleagues and former students, both white and BIPOC, whose challenge, love and support made this book possible. Your names are too many to list, but I hope you know how you have impacted me. Finally, I am grateful to my wife Cynthia, who continues to support me in my effort to make a positive contribution for racial justice in our world.

Introduction

To get to a point where race won't make a difference,
we have to wrestle, first, with the difference that race makes.
                                                    —Michael Eric Dyson

Charlottesville, Virginia, August 2017

On August 11, 2017, a group of self-proclaimed white nationalists marched through the campus of the University of Virginia carrying lit tiki torches, chanting and signs that read "White Lives Matter," "You Will Not Replace Us" and the Nazi-inspired phrase, "Blood and Soil." Counter-protestors gathered to challenge their presence and some scattered brawls ensued. Police soon arrived and dispersed the crowd.

Both groups were in Charlottesville for the highly publicized "Unite the Right" rally that was scheduled for the next day, Saturday, August 12th. The white nationalists had come to protest a decision made several months earlier by the Charlottesville City Council to remove a statue of the Confederate General Robert E. Lee from a public park. This decision was part of a movement in many southern U.S. cities to remove memorials to the Confederate cause and the overt racism they symbolized. In May 2017, several months after the Council decision, a group of about 100 white nationalists, led by well-known white-nationalist leader Richard Spencer, staged a protest. A month later the park was renamed Emancipation Park. This then led to a white-nationalist call for the "Unite the Right" rally.

On the morning of August 12th, a group about 500 protestors from various white-nationalist and far-right groups gathered at Emancipation Park. Richard Spencer and David Duke were present, as were visibly armed, right-wing militia groups claiming to be there to protect the demonstrators' First Amendment rights. However, before the rally could begin, they were met by approximately 1000 counter-protestors, including an interfaith gathering of clergy who had come to Charlottesville from across the country, representatives of various progressive groups and unions, ordinary citizens from the local area and members of Antifa, a network of militant anti-fascist and leftist groups committed to direct action against white nationalists.[1]

The protestors waved Confederate flags and chanted anti-Semitic and racist slogans. The counter-protestors were led by a group of about 20 clergy who had linked arms and were praying and singing peace songs. Very quickly the standoff turned violent with people on both sides kicking, punching, hurling water bottles and spraying chemicals. The local police were present, but remained largely pulled back from the gathering while the chaotic conflict escalated. At 11 a.m., a state of emergency was declared and riot police attempted to disperse the crowd. Instead, the protest and conflicts simply moved from the park to city streets. At 1:45 that afternoon, a white-nationalist protestor drove his car into a crowd of counter-protestors, hitting several people including 32-year-old Charlottesville resident Heather Heyer, who later died. Fourteen other people were sent to the hospital with serious injuries.[2]

Where Were the White People? Where Are the White People?

While all of this was going on, I was on vacation across the country in Oregon. I had gone there to visit other family members and to enjoy the beautiful mountains and beaches of that state. As was my custom when on vacation, I purposely limited my exposure to national and global news. I was aware that something was brewing in Charlottesville, but admittedly had not paid much attention to what it was actually all about. However, when I returned home a few days after the confrontation, I was shocked and disturbed by what had occurred and quickly attempted to learn all I could about the tragic events in Charlottesville.[3]

Equally disturbing for me was the relative lack of response from the white community. While various persons and leaders of color were speaking out against the overt racism involved in the "Unite the Right" rally, very few white people and leaders spoke up against its racist intent. President

Trump, when asked about his response, equivocated by saying, "I think there was blame on both sides," and later clarified his remarks by saying that "not all the people [at the rally] were neo-Nazis ... [or] white supremacists by any stretch." This was an interesting statement given that it was a rally publicly called by white nationalists.

Now to be fair, there were many white clergy present in Charlottesville who showed up and spoke; most of the Antifa there were white and the deceased Heather Heyer was white. However, mainstream white America was largely silent or, in many cases, openly resistant to any suggestion that the white nationalists had done anything fundamentally wrong. Most white Americans simply saw that and other such events as something that did not affect or involve them. Some, like the president, saw it as a clash between two rowdy groups, equally culpable for the chaos and death that ensued. Moreover, in my own attempts to engage other white people to discuss the events in Charlottesville, I was met with anger, silence or defensiveness.

Why I Wrote This Book
The aftermath of Charlottesville impressed upon me that white people by and large don't know how to constructively talk about race. After the shooting of Michael Brown in Ferguson, Missouri; after Dylan Roof murdered nine members of Emanuel AME church in Charleston, South Carolina; after George Zimmerman was acquitted for the shooting of Trayvon Martin; and countless other times, so many white people in my circles had nothing to say. Some saw no relevance of these events to their lives, some were defensive and some were just afraid to say anything for fear of being accused as "racist." Moreover, I have found in predominantly white social settings that the topic of race is usually met with blank stares or a change of topic. Those who are white so often don't want and or know how to talk about race. It must be noted that in the protests following the deaths of George Floyd, Breonna Taylor and Ahmaud Arbery, whites joined in numbers that were unprecedented for issues related to race. Yet even so, the vast majority of whites looked in fear and silence.

The purpose of this book is to address this deficit; simply put, it's to help those who are concerned about the rising tide of overt and covert racism in U.S. society to have conversations about these issues with white co-workers, friends, acquaintances and family members. For over 40 years, I have been involved in various forms of antiracist and social-justice work, very often alongside Black, Indigenous and People of Color (BIPOC). The effort to incorporate antiracism into all aspects of my life and work has been a significant part of my personal and professional development. At the same time, I recognize that I am far from free of the attitudes, ignorance and indifference of most white people I know. In so doing, I not only share my insights, but also my questions and struggles.

Over the years, I have heard my friends and colleagues of color repeatedly say that white people can't solely depend on BIPOC to make them aware of and teach them about racism. Repeatedly, these colleagues say that whites "need to do their own work." Having said that, like many white people, most of what I have learned about the impact and destructiveness of racism on individual lives and whole communities has come from teachers, colleagues and students of color who have had the courage to make me aware of how my words or actions have reflected an overt or implicit racial bias. I have made it part of my own professional growth to read extensively about the impact of racism on various dimensions of our society and, more often than not, those authors have also been BIPOC. In recent years, white authors such as Tim Wise,[4] Robin DiAngelo,[5] Paul Kivel,[6] Jeff Hitchcock[7] and others have highlighted the ways in which—personally, culturally and institutionally—whites in this country have benefited by, propagated and yet remained largely unconscious of the various ways white supremacy and whiteness has and continues to shape their daily lives. I have come to see that we who are white need to address the ways in which the white-supremacist system in which we live has socialized us, and to transform ourselves as we also work to change the racist structures and systems in our society.

Yet all the attention that has recently been focused on racism has only seemed to heighten the anxiety and powerlessness that many well-meaning whites feel. In my courses, workshops and other settings, I have often listened to white people bemoan the difficulty of talking with friends and family members about current events having to do with race-related concerns. The authors and authorities referenced above have done a good job of identifying and analyzing the problem of whiteness and white supremacy in our individual lives and society at large, but for the most part have been short on how to address the problem. Largely missing is a discussion of how whites can talk to other whites about these issues. The subtitle of Robin DiAngelo's 2018 book, *White Fragility*, captures the dilemma well: *Why It's So Hard for White People to Talk About Racism*.[8] There is a growing cohort of whites who have come to affirm that white supremacy is a critical problem that needs to be addressed, but are not sure how to approach it—especially with close friends and family members.

Disrupting Whiteness takes up the challenge implied in DiAngelo's subtitle, to move the conversation about whites and racism from simply acknowledgment of the problem to a discussion of how we can constructively engage our white friends and family members in meaningful and potentially transformative conversations about racism. In order to do that, I build on the work of all those others, both whites and BIPOC, who have highlighted the issues that whites need to address first in themselves and then in others, and to propose concrete positive responses.

Disrupting Whiteness

Although racism has been part of the American story since its beginnings, white people have been socialized to believe that race has nothing to do with them, that it's a problem for others to address. As a result, most white people never talk about race, except when something affects them directly and that is usually not often. Whites have not been socialized to think critically about race in general, but particularly about themselves as racialized persons. Instead, most whites don't see themselves as having a race, unless in a situation where they are a racial minority.

Consequently, most whites don't see themselves in racial terms and therefore "don't carry the psychic weight of race" or "have to worry about how others feel about [their] race."[9] Racism doesn't impede where one can go, what options one has, and rarely limits access to people with social and political connections and other things of importance. Additionally, there is little awareness that there are many things whites take for granted that are denied to BIPOC. Moreover, in most predominantly white groups and settings, there is an unspoken agreement that whites won't do or say anything that will cause anyone to feel discomfort because of race. DiAngelo refers to this silent contract as "white solidarity," calling it "the unspoken agreement among whites to protect white advantage and not cause another white person racial discomfort by confronting them when they say or do something that is racially problematic."[10] The key to white solidarity is silence about topics that suggest whites have some sort of social or racial advantage. So at family gatherings, meet-and-greets and other social settings, when someone says or does something overtly racist, excuses are made for the behavior or the person is given a pass as "he is really a nice person." And if someone dares to broach the R-word, generally people withdraw, as if nothing was said. I have actually gone to such settings and brought up the topic of race, surprised at how quickly the subject changes. But I have also been in circumstances where an overtly racist comment was made and found myself frozen, not knowing what to say, unable to speak. Like most of the white people I know, I have been properly socialized into the rules of white solidarity.

However, in this book I am choosing to break those rules and talk openly about racism—my own experiences and struggles and those of my fellow white people. Moreover, I am inviting both whites and BIPOC to break the code of silence around white solidarity. In essence, I am calling upon you, the reader, to join me in disrupting whiteness in all its forms, and instead talk openly and honestly with the white people in your life.

An Outline of the Book

A working assumption in this book is that no white person in the U.S. context can contend that they are free of racism. As Robin DiAngelo has so clearly said: "Only white people can be racist and all whites are racist."[11] I know for some that assumption is a hard pill to swallow, but it has to do with what we understand racism to be and how whites became captive to racism. What I seek to prescribe is a process whereby whites are working to address their internalized racism while seeking to engage other whites to join them in that process. The book begins with a section titled "Knowing Your Race Story;" before one engages in talking with others about the impact of racism in their lives, an awareness of the impact of racism on one's own life must be developed. So I begin describing a way that one can identify and reflect on the influences and incidents in their life that have shaped their understanding of race and racism. To assist in that process, I provide a working understanding of terms like racism, white privilege, white supremacy, implicit bias and whiteness. I then discuss how white supremacy has not only caused untold suffering to BIPOC, but also has hurt white people in profound ways and led to white fragility. I then explore the history of race and racism in America, highlighting three key themes of that history.

Throughout this first section, the purpose is to assist readers in understanding the complex and myriad ways that racism, white supremacy and whiteness (three terms I use somewhat interchangeably) have shaped their behavior, attitudes, emotions and perceptions in everyday life. In this way, readers are able to understand the ongoing effort to resist and overcome the effect of racism in their own lives, even as they challenge others to do the same.

The second section of the book, "Engaging White People About Racism," focuses on many of the responses that white people give when the topic of race is broached. I suggest an approach involving personal storytelling, active listening and dialogue. I learned this through my involvement in a monthly interracial, interfaith gathering called NewCORE (New Conversations on Race and Ethnicity). What we have learned at NewCORE is that when people tell their story, they often see and hear things in that story they had not previously recognized. This storytelling is followed by asking probing questions that seek to draw other people out and cause them to look more deeply into what they have come to believe about their experience.[12] This leads to dialogue among all involved about the way we think and respond about racially charged events.

Having outlined this dialogical approach, I then address several common responses whites give when the topic of racism is broached, such as claiming to be colorblind, denying racial privilege, asserting historical and personal innocence, bringing up instances of so-called reverse racism, attempting to deflect the conversation and responding with anger. I also discuss the tendency of more progressive whites to think of themselves as some sort of saviors. I offer ideas gleaned from my and others' experiences interrupting overtly racist statements and actions. In each chapter, I provide background on the various responses whites give to the topic of racism and then offer ways to enter into conversation around those responses.

The final chapter calls on whites to quit ignoring and ducking the issue of racism and take responsibility for their growth in this area of their life. The book concludes with a simple recognition that addressing racism in our lives and society is not a quick fix but requires us to take the long view, relentlessly committed to the work for racial justice.

In 2015, I published a book titled *White Allies in the Struggle for Racial Justice,* whose purpose is to provide role models of white people throughout U.S. history who sought to work in solidarity with African Americans to achieve racial justice in their time. I described allies as people who had come to "recognize that a world free of oppression is one of dignity, equality, humanity and justice, and therefore is a better world for all people regardless of their social position."[13] Allyship, as I described it, involves white people physically and actively joining Black people and other BIPOC in their resistance to oppression and struggles for liberation.[14] What I have come to realize since writing that book is that allyship also involves white people confronting and challenging other whites to recognize and accept the ways in which white supremacy has shaped their lives and the systems that shape our history, culture and institutions. In so doing, they can move their fellow whites from defensiveness and resistance to openness and active support of efforts to eradicate the racial injustices that exist.

The Confession of a Recovering Racist

Let me make clear that I don't write this book as an expert on how to talk to white people about race, or as one who has overcome all of his internal and external racism; I am still very much a work in progress. Whenever I address the topic of racism or what I have come to call white supremacy,[15] I always begin with a confession: *I am a recovering racist.* What I mean is that I am the product of a family, a community and a national culture that led me to believe that my experience as a middle-class, white, heterosexual male is the same experience as that of all persons regardless of race, gender, class or sexual orientation. Moreover, I was raised to believe that the success I had in life was solely the result of my intelligence and hard work. I grew up believing that the education system, the criminal-justice system, the government and other institutions in U.S. society, while not perfect, sought to operate in a fair and impartial manner when it came to race. And so whatever I achieved and learned I believed was the result of my playing by the rules and working hard.

I didn't realize that the game was rigged in my favor and I had been socialized to believe that I was a little bit smarter, a little bit more resilient and therefore a little bit better than many others. And I did not think it due to our race that most of the people who achieved in areas I did were white, but to our superior effort. Racism was bred into me from the day I was born by loving parents, diligent teachers and other caring role models without my knowing and most likely without their knowing either. Like a child born into a drug-infested environment, I was bound to become addicted to the drug of white superiority. Much of my personal journey toward an antiracist lifestyle has involved unlearning my privilege and limited worldview, and relearning a new way of seeing and living in the world.

At the same time I confess my inherited racism, I also call myself a *recovering* racist. In the 12-step movements like Alcoholics Anonymous, Gamblers Anonymous and Narcotics Anonymous, when people complete a 12-step program they never say they are recover*ed*; rather they say they are recover*ing*. The genius of the 12-step movement is that it recognizes one is never free of addiction, but instead must continually work on one's recovery. The minute they begin to think they are "over it," they begin to slide back into their addiction. In the same way, while I have learned and grown a great deal in regard to my own racism over the last several decades, I have been reminded more times than I care to count that I still have work to do. Every time I teach a class or lead a discussion on race, I purposely turn the light on myself before I challenge others to look at themselves. In the same way, in this book I turn the light on myself and examine my own interactions with whites (and often failures to do so constructively), as I seek to share what I have learned about how to talk about race-related issues with my fellow whites.

In characterizing myself in this manner, I am not engaging in self-flagellation. Too often when white folks hear the word "racism," they feel they are being accused of something horrible and unforgiveable. In some cases that may be true. However, I propose that racism is not an accusation but a diagnosis of our lives as white men and women, and a description of the racially tainted and discriminatory society in which we live. If a man is sick and goes to the doctor, he receives a diagnosis and description of his condition before treatment is prescribed. In the same manner, if white people in the United States are ever going to overcome racism in themselves and in society at large, they first must come to terms with the reality that they are racially tainted people in a society soaking with racism from top to bottom.

This book is written for white people who have come to deplore the scourge of racism in their lives and society, and who are in relationship with other whites who don't share their deep concern for how racism is so endemic to every aspect of American life. They recognize, like themselves, that their white friends grew up in a largely white bubble and were socialized to not understand the effect of white supremacy on their lives. This book is also for BIPOC who have not yet given up on their white friends and who want to help them move forward in their growing commitment to an antiracist lifestyle. Moreover, this book attempts to facilitate a conversation about how whites can move beyond guilt, powerlessness, frustration and defensiveness toward a more racially constructive way of thinking, and seeks to move the reader toward a supportive engagement of the white people in their lives as they contend with the racism in our culture, institutions and systems. As I point out throughout the book, this is not an easy path to follow; it's what Scott Peck calls a "road less traveled,"[16] but is the right road, nonetheless. I invite you, the reader, to join me on this journey.

Section 1

Knowing Your Race Story

What Is Your Race Story?

*When we deny the story, it defines us. When we own
the story, we can write a brave new ending.*

—Brene Brown

Starting with Ourselves

If we who are white want to resist, undo and overcome the impact of racism in American society, we must start with ourselves. For that reason, whites must begin by probing and understanding their own experiences with regard to race. For many years I have taught college classes and led workshops on racism. In those settings I often begin by asking people to reflect on what I call their "race story." I begin by asking them to reflect on a few basic questions to encourage people to think about their socialization around issues of race and then to ask themselves how those experiences shaped and influenced them. Anyone who has spent time in the United States, whether born here or immigrated, has been influenced by dynamics of race. However, many white people in this country don't think of themselves in racial terms. While they think of other groups of people as having a race, many whites have not been socialized to think of themselves as having a race. In fact, for many whites, it's only when they encounter BIPOC that they begin to think of themselves in terms of being white.

The questions listed below invite one to reflect on what it means to be a racialized person and how that impacts interactions and relationships with others. If engaging white people in a discussion about how racism has shaped and impacted them, a person needs to know his or her own race story.

The questions are as follows.

1. *How would you describe your race?* This assumes in our society every person has been racialized and either has been categorized racially by others and/or has chosen to identify racially in a particular way. For many white people, this may not be a question they have seriously considered.

2. *When did you first become aware of race as something to be concerned about?* This invites one to reflect when the topic of race was introduced. It may have been something seen on the news, something encountered outside the home, or something discussed by one's parents or other significant adults. Important with this question is the feeling tone or underlying message associated with one's awareness. In many white homes, the topic of race itself was considered taboo, something not talked about at all or only in code. In other cases, race may have been a common topic, only in overtly derogatory ways.

3. *When did you first become aware of your race?* Sometimes the answer to this question is the same as that for the previous question. However, for many people, especially white people, one first becomes aware of others' race. For some, becoming aware that one has a race is a shocking and disturbing reality, especially if socialized not to talk about it.

4. *When did you first become aware of racism?* For many white people, racism is something that happens to a distant other, or someone might have grown up in an environment where racist attitudes, actions and words were commonly spoken, but unaware that was overtly racist. I once had an adult student who insisted that racism was not part of her upbringing. Then she remembered her grandfather coming home and taking off his white hood and robe. Until that point, she had no idea of the racist environment in which she had been raised.

5. *When was the first time you witnessed or experienced racism?* This gets at when racism became personal, when it was no longer an idea, but something one had seen, heard or experienced. When experiencing racism in a personal way, it becomes more real. Many whites

will only have indirectly seen or heard something they understood as racist.

6. *What, if any, messages do you remember being given about race and/ or racism by your parents, teachers and other significant adults in your childhood?* This allows one to reflect on the subtle and not-so-subtle messages significant others gave about race and racism while growing up.

7. *If you know something of your family history, when were your ancestors first considered white on the North American continent? What were they seen as before considered white? What was lost when they became white?* With the increased tracing of family histories, these questions invite one to consider what it means to be called "white." Many immigrants such as Jews, Irish and East Europeans were—upon arrival—discriminated against, but over time gained the power and privilege of whiteness through assimilation. This ability was never fully available to many darker-skinned people groups.[1]

8. *What are some critical incidents in your life where the reality of racism became clear to you and showed something about yourself and the world around you that which you had not previously realized?* This focus on critical incidents seeks to identify events, relationships and other situations that made people aware of their own attitudes and emotions regarding race, and caused them either to withdraw and become defensive, or to change their behavior, worldview and attitudes about BIPOC. These incidents can often be disturbing and it may not be until much later in life that people realize the full impact that racism had on their lives.

From these questions, people can begin to construct their "race story." The questions are meant to be evocative, opening them up to consider the ways they have been shaped by the people and events in their lives. In my classes and workshops, as people reflect on and answer these questions, I then gently probe in order to understand more fully the context of their experiences, what were they feeling, what changed for them and how it affected them going forward. I also ask them to think about what else may have been going on at the time that may have contributed to their experiences.

Once whites understand their race story, it becomes a foundation and resource for talking about racism with other whites. Being able to acknowledge that one has had uncomfortable feelings or thoughts in conversations about racism allows a person to find common ground with others' with the same struggle. From that point, one can then share how working through the experience was more racially constructive.

For instance, an adult student of mine was once reading a book by an African American author critical of white male professors who fail to acknowledge their need for cultural competency. He was offended by the author's assertion and felt she was out "to make white men like him feel guilty." I shared with him that I had sometimes felt similarly in situations where white male dominance was being called out. I went on to say that I came to see the author's assertion (not accusation) was often true and caused me to look at myself. This then led to a more extensive discussion of how often white males are oblivious to their privilege and dismissal of BIPOC.

My Race Story

By way of illustrating how this process works, let me share pieces of my race story. As previously indicated, I grew up in an upper middle class, suburban community outside Minneapolis, Minnesota. All of my friends, teachers and other significant influences were white. Since it was the 1960s, I was aware of the Civil Rights Movement primarily through the television news media. My parents did not talk about what was going on; it was just not a topic of discussion. In any case, it was something happening down South and did not concern us in the North. Where I heard about racism and race issues was in church, where the pastor frequently mentioned racism and civil rights in his sermons. In other ways, racism was subtly part of my upbringing. On the playground we used to pick up teams by counting "eenie, meenie, miney, mo, catch a n----r by the toe." We referred to Japanese and Jewish people in derogatory terms. We thought of Black people in terms of "Little Black Sambo."

When I was 10 years old, I had my first encounter with a person of another race. I was running around a city park and met a Black boy my age. He had a strong southern accent and I could not understand him. I remember thinking of him as different and strange. In high school I learned about the Civil Rights Movement in a history class, but it wasn't until I went to college in North Carolina that racism became real to me.

During my first year there, I volunteered to tutor children at a small African American church about a mile off campus. Usually we were driven there by a professor, but one evening our driver could not make it, so we walked. As we followed the road to the church, at a particular point the road continued but the pavement stopped and became a dirt road. We had entered the Black community and it dawned on me: "Oh, this is what segregation is." Around that same time, I attended an all-white church, where the pastor's wife gave an impassioned plea to fight efforts by the city school system to integrate the public schools; it struck me again—aha—that this is what segregation is about. Shortly after that, I met a young Black man who was best friends with the son of a white Methodist minister. He shared with me a painful experience of being refused entrance to his friend's church when he went there to worship. Through many similar experiences, I was introduced to the way racial discrimination and segregation were woven into the fabric of life and that the Black people in the\at uno\iversity town were clearly treated as second-class citizens. Though I still understood very little, it awakened in me a desire to do something about racism and I decided to do urban youthwork.

Upon graduation from college, I went to work with a youth ministry organization in a reputably liberal northern city. When I arrived, the city was in an uproar. A federal judge had ordered the city's school district to desegregate its schools. Rocks were being thrown at school buses, people were being dragged out of their cars and beaten, and neighborhoods (including mine) were cordoned off by police barricades. This was the first personal encounter I had with the vitriol, hatred and violence of racism. In my southern college town, racism was just part of the fabric of the culture, but in that northern city, racism was overt, unapologetic and violent. Contrary to what I had been raised to believe, racism was not just a "southern thing," but was very much alive in the North as well.

7

In telling and exploring my story, I have had to ask why my community growing up was all white? Why was the focus on the South's racism and not on that in the North? What forces were at play in my university community that clearly divided people along racial lines? What was the source of the hatred witnessed in that northern city? And how was I part of it all?

Knowing Our Story Opens Up Others

In this book I will share many of the critical, eye-opening, often gut-wrenching incidents that have shaped me. By reflecting on my own story and probing these experiences, I have come to a much fuller understanding of how my life has been and continues to be shaped by the racial dynamics in our society. Moreover, I have come to understand how the racial dynamics at work in our nation's history continue to affect me and the white people in my life. This awareness has made me vigilant. And it keeps me humble.

Too often, conversations about race devolve into name-calling and defensiveness. Too often, white people who want to challenge and fight racism come across as thinking themselves superior and judgmental. In reality, none of us are free of racism's influence in the past or present. At best, some are just more aware and trying to resist and overcome those racist influences. Knowing and owning our race stories keeps us humble. Knowing the impact that history has and still has on us keeps us humble. That humility and openness to continuous growth can then provide the foundation for helping other white people understand the impact that racial dynamics have on them as well.

Facing Discomfort

While becoming aware of the ways racism has impacted one's life can be eye-opening, it also can be extremely uncomfortable. Beneath all of the ways that white people avoid, deny and fight the reality of racism, its impact on them is discomfort. Talking about race, confronting the racism in one's own life and seeking to help others see racism in themselves can be exhausting, embarrassing, awkward and just plain difficult. Facing and dealing with racism in oneself, in others one cares about and in the society in which we live is hard work. Though difficult, I believe the fruits of that work can be redemptive for all involved.

It's necessary work. For too long, white people have had the privilege to not deal with racism either personally or institutionally. As the United States continues to diversify and the globe becomes increasingly interconnected, whites no longer have the luxury of avoiding discussions about race and racism. That process must begin with those who say they are committed to combatting racism, who claim to be "woke." So let us begin....

What Do We Mean by Race and Racism?

*Racism is still with us. But it's up to us to prepare our children
for what they have to meet and hopefully, we shall overcome.*
—Rosa Parks

The Case of Steve King

In January 2019, Representative Steve King, a nine-term Republican Congressman from Iowa, was stripped of his seats on the House of Representatives committees by the Republican leadership. In a 424-1 vote, Rep. King was also rebuked by his colleagues in both parties. What was the offense? A few days earlier in an interview with *The New York Times*, King was quoted as saying, "White Nationalist, white Supremacist, Western civilization—how did that language become offensive?" For years he had been quoted publicly promoting white nationalist views and disparaging Muslims, Central American immigrants and BIPOC. Yet this public endorsement of white nationalism (which King later denied) had apparently gone too far.[1]

However, King's overt racism was nothing new. In fact, his public record indicates clear and coded racist remarks going back as far as 2002. What King said that fateful day in the *Times* interview would not have caught anyone familiar with the congressman by surprise. He had been saying such things and advocating racist policies for years. The question is not why King said what he did nor why his colleagues censured him, but why he was not censured earlier. In some cases, it might be that King's colleagues quietly shared his views, but did not speak out publicly. However, my guess is that many others may have seen King's comments as annoying but still just his opinion and so not able to be challenged.

However, at a much more foundational level the case of King is not as unique as it may seem and, in fact, points to a profound misunderstanding of the concept of race and racism. Numerous polls have indicated that, in varying degrees, most Americans believe racism is still a problem in our country, but no polls I am aware of have asked them to describe or define what racism is. If asked, I suspect that most people, especially whites, understand racism to be discriminatory acts or speech directed at persons of another race or ethnicity. For that reason, many whites will cite instances where they themselves were the targets of what has often been called "reverse racism." Later in this book I will explore this claim of reverse racism. What I want to stress in this chapter is that most white people think racism is something that happens between two people or groups who happen to be of different races and, as long as people don't do or say anything discriminatory against another person, they cannot be accused of being racist. By that definition, King's error was not that he held certain views about people of nonwhite racial groups, but that he voiced them in a public setting. If Rep. King had not spoken up, or at least spoken so openly and publicly, he would still have his committee assignments and would not have been labeled as racist by his colleagues in Congress.

While Rep. King's views and words can be considered racially objectionable, this view of racism is far too narrow and prevents many white people from grasping the pervasiveness of racism and white supremacy in all aspects of U.S. society. A broader understanding is needed before we can talk meaningfully with other white people about the impact of racism on their lives.

What Is Race?

Before we can talk intelligently about racism, we need to understand what we mean by the term "race." Most academic discussions today on the meaning and nature of race are based on the groundbreaking work of sociologists Michael Omi and Howard Winant in their book, *Racial Formation in the United States*;[2] this book's discussion on the nature of race will draw heavily from it. While race and racism have been shaped by a centuries-long conflict between white domination and BIPOC resistance to that domination, the concept of "racial identity is a slippery thing" continues to evolve and change. What is constant throughout is that race has always been tied to the experiences of difference, inequality and how people understand themselves as individuals and groups.[3]

Race and racial conflict has been part of the American story from the moment Europeans landed on the shores of North America and encountered the indigenous people living there, and then those same Europeans imported millions of African captives to work as slaves. The meaning and significance of race is enshrined in the Declaration of Independence,[4] U.S. Constitution[5] and other national founding documents. The significance of race gave rise to a protracted struggle between those who sought to preserve slavery and those who fought to abolish it, eventually leading to the devastating Civil War, the legacy of which still impacts American life today. Race was at the heart of the westward expansion of European settlers, the displacement and genocide of millions of indigenous persons, and the appropriation of lands in what is now the American southwest. Race continued to be defined and refined as immigrants from parts of Eastern and southern Europe were first excluded and then assimilated as white, even as Asian and South American immigrants found that enfranchisement harder to attain. Race gave rise to the dynamic Civil Rights Movement in the mid-20th century, which itself inspired liberation movements among other racially marginalized groups. Race has influenced political strategy, economic policy, educational opportunity, healthcare availability, and protracted violence and discrimination throughout U.S. history; in other words, race has always been at the heart of the American story and is still central to daily life today.

Race as a Social Construct

Many people tend to think of race in terms of physical characteristics such as skin color, facial features, types of hair and the like, but that is overly simplistic. For instance, the singer Alicia Keys, who is light-skinned with aquiline features, and actor Chris Rock, whose skin is much darker, are both considered Black. This is because race has to do with more than physical features.

From the 15th to the 20th centuries, race was primarily understood as essentially physically and biologically based. Several attempts were made by scientists to distinguish various racial groups on the basis of brain

13

size, facial features, body type, geographical location and essential human nature. Throughout much of U.S. history, race was considered to be determined by the nature of one's blood. In large part, these distinctions were pursued in an effort to prove whites were the superior race. However, with the emergence of the Human Genome Project and subsequent research, all efforts to identify and distinguish racial and ethnic groups on the basis of their physical and genetic makeup were abandoned. One simply could not identify a person's race on the basis of their features and DNA. As biologist David Unander states, "Genetically, we all belong to highly smudged categories within one human race."[6]

An individual's race is ultimately determined by how he or she is perceived by their society and how they choose to identify themselves. We call this a social construct. Drawing on the work of Omi and Winant, I define race as *a socially constructed identity, where the content and importance of racial categories are determined by social, economic and political forces.* They state that "race is a master category—a fundamental concept that has profoundly shaped and continues to shape the history, policy, economic structure and culture of the United States."[7]

While some white nationalists argue that there are biological or culturally irreconcilable differences between persons of different racial groups, overwhelmingly the idea that race is a social construct is widely accepted by scholars in the field. A social construct is an idea, a concept or understanding of the world that has been created and given significance by society. This construct shapes people's lives and gives them a sense of meaning and direction, which emerges from the values and beliefs important to a group, which differ from culture to culture and society.

Let me give a simple example: I am a devoted fan of the Philadelphia Eagles professional football team. Between the months of August and February, my schedule is oriented around theirs, and my emotions rise and fall with their wins and losses. There are some Eagles fans who spend thousands of dollars each season to attend games and even travel across the country to watch them play. There are radio and TV stations, phone apps, retail clothing stores and other establishments whose businesses are largely or totally dedicated to promoting the Eagles. Fans say they "bleed Eagles green." And, of course, the players themselves are paid millions of dollars to feed and fulfill the passion of their fans.

The Philadelphia Eagles and its fans are social constructs. Over the years, the players come and go, the coaches come and go, the executives and managers come and go; what remain are the Eagles organization and its fans. The social construct of the Eagles has a profound impact on hundreds of thousands of lives and, while those people may differ economically, politically, culturally and geographically, they are bound together by that construct. Those fans see themselves as a discrete group and are perceived by others not part of their group as a unique collection of football-crazed individuals.

So it's with race as a social construct; while race cannot be biologically determined, it's real because generations of Americans have made it a reality in our national life. U.S. history has been and continues to be shaped by how people perceive those whom they consider racial others. As Omi and Winant state: "Race is not something rooted in nature, something that reflects clear and discrete variations in human identity. But race is not an illusion ... race is indeed real as a social category with definite social consequences."[8]

Through a process called racialization, perceived racial differences are given meaning and social value. Various character traits, behavioral tendencies, cultural idiosyncrasies and social values are attributed to certain groups of people perceived to be part of a particular racial group.[9] Those attributes in turn influence the way people in various racial groups interact with one another. Racialization can also lump together various culturally distinct groups who don't see themselves as similar and yet are categorized as a specific racial group. So, for instance, today we may talk about Asian Americans or Hispanics, yet within those racialized groups are wide cultural and behavioral distinctions. For example, groups who are of Japanese and Chinese descent see themselves quite differently, while racially they are categorized as Asian. Likewise, one may be considered Hispanic or Latinx and yet be Mexican, Puerto Rican or Cuban, all quite culturally distinct groups. The racialized group referred to as Black can culturally be identified as African American, Caribbean or African.

In and of themselves, these racial categories are neither bad nor good, but when given greater or lesser social value—and those who are most powerful and dominant in society begin to make decisions, pass laws, establish institutions, provide access to resources and generally structure society based on those race-based social values—then racism emerges.

Racism

As illustrated in the story of Representative Steve King, racism is often perceived as disparaging thoughts, words and behaviors by a person of one racial group toward another. While those words and actions can be construed as racist, such an understanding is limited and highly oversimplified. Simply talking or acting negatively toward persons of another racial group in itself is not necessarily racist. Such actions might be a form of prejudice but not necessarily racist. So first we must distinguish racial prejudice from racism.

DiAngelo describes racial prejudice as a "prejudgment about another person based on the social groups to which a person belongs. Prejudice consists of thoughts and feelings, including stereotypes, attitudes and generalizations that are based on little or no experience and then are projected onto everyone from that group."[10] All people have prejudice; it's often a shorthand way of seeking to understand other people and can break down when people have meaningful personal contact with others. For instance, as a Philadelphia Eagles fan, I am very prejudiced against fans of the Dallas Cowboys, but that prejudice has been weakened by my personal contact with specific Dallas fans.

Prejudice becomes racism when a particular group has social, political, cultural or economic power to discriminate or dominate the actions and opportunities of another group. As that ability gets normalized and regulated, it then becomes consistently enacted. Racism can be defined as *a political, economic, cultural and structural system that consistently advantages one group over another on the basis of the racial identification.* As DiAngelo states: "When a group's collective prejudice is backed by the power of legal authority and institutional control, it's transformed into a racism."[11] In effect, the racial prejudices of the dominant racial group become institutionalized and therefore can operate without the conscious intentions of those benefiting from that prejudice. Furthermore, individuals in the dominant racial group can speak and act in a racist manner without full awareness of the power that allows them to do such things.[12]

The key difference between prejudice and racism is power. When an individual or collective group has the power to enact their prejudice in concrete and specific ways, that prejudice becomes racism. The exercise of power can be intentional and personal, as when a teacher disciplines a student of color more harshly than a white student. Or the exercise of power can be more broadly institutional or systemic, such that the racial preference is embedded in laws, policies and practices that favor whites over BIPOC. Returning again to the example of Steven King, his actions and words were particularly egregious because of his powerful position as a U.S. congressman. He not only held a position of great authority, he had the capacity to pass laws that could significantly impact millions of people whom his words demeaned.

Dimensions of Racism

When we talk about racism, we need to recognize that it exists in four different dimensions: the internalized, interpersonal, institutional and systemic. Each of these has their own way of degrading, excluding, marginalizing and injuring BIPOC As people consider their race story, they must reflect on how these different dimensions influenced perceptions, shaped attitudes, perpetuated falsehoods and guided behaviors both in mixed-race and all-white settings. While becoming aware of these dimensions in one's life can be eye-opening, they can also be deeply disturbing. The challenge is to see how racism has shaped us and not run away from the truth we see.

Internalized Racism

The first aspect of racism and least outwardly visible is the *internalized* dimension. This is the area of one's thoughts and feelings dictating personal behavior and perspectives. For white people, internalized racism takes the form of an inner sense of superiority, both conscious and unconscious. This feeling can be malevolent, such as seeing BIPOC as somehow deficient or less than oneself. But the sense of superiority can also show itself in a form of pity for people who are considered "less fortunate." The common denominator in both expressions of internalized racism is that, as a white person, one views him/herself as somehow greater, better or more advanced than BIPOC.[13] This internalized racism can also cause one to feel uncomfortable in a racially diverse group or where one is numerically the racial minority, because in such settings the white person doesn't have as much control. And a result, one might withdraw or remove themselves from the setting based on some non-racial excuse. Having faced that uncomfortable feeling, in the future the white people may well decide to avoid such gatherings, because they have a need to feel superior and more in charge.

The images and stereotypes that lead to certain thoughts and feelings are often inherited by one's parents and significant others early in childhood. While one may have a traumatic or emotional experience leading to certain racist stereotypes, more often than not the racist feelings and stereotypes are absorbed by messages one receives from the day of birth. I have been doing antiracism and reconciliation work for nearly 40 years and yet I confess that I still find stereotypes and fears about people of other racial groups arising in me in confounding and troubling ways. While I have worked intentionally to change my inner thoughts and emotions, they are so deeply embedded in my psyche that, despite my best efforts, they will occasionally emerge. The challenge in this internalized dimension of racism is how one responds. While people may not be able to totally eradicate the racist images and messages they received growing up, they can choose not to allow them to control their behavior and interactions with others.

Internalized racism takes another form with BIPOC in that they can feel "less than" simply because they are not white: less intelligent, less attractive, less capable and less valuable because they are Black or Brown. When one lives in a society that daily conveys messages of BIPOC as somehow deficient, one can begin to believe those messages. Internalized racism shows up in jokes people tell, standards they set for themselves and in the way in which BIPOC not only devalue themselves but each other.[14]

Perhaps the most pernicious form of internalized racism among BIPOC is colorism, a prejudice in Black and Brown communities where those with a darker hue to their skin are seen as less acceptable than those with lighter skin. Just as white people prefer those with white or light skin, so too BIPOC will sometimes prefer light to darker skin. Employers tend to prefer lighter-skinned African Americans, and lighter-skinned Latinx and Filipinos earn higher wages than those with darker skin. The color standard set by the dominant white culture gets adopted by BIPOC themselves. Lighter-skinned women are seen as more attractive and darker-skinned men more dangerous.[15]

With both whites and BIPOC, racism begins with how one's inner thoughts and feelings influence behavior toward oneself and people of other races. Thus, while not being as outwardly evident as other dimensions of racism, internalized racism in many ways is the root from which the other dimensions emerge, grow and develop.

Interpersonal Racism

This leads us to the second dimension of racism, which is the *interpersonal*, which deals with how persons interact with those whom they perceive as racially different from themselves and how they talk about those persons when they are with people whom they perceive to be part of their racial group.

1. Overt Racism

When most people consider whether a person is racist, they think of overt racism: the use of certain racially derogatory words and obvious displays of racially discriminatory symbols and actions that are harmful toward people of nonwhite racial or ethnic groups. Longitudinal studies have shown that, over the past several decades, whites have had a "dramatic increase in support for principles of racial equality—things like support for equality in jobs, schools and public accommodations."[16] The data also shows that significantly fewer whites endorse negative stereotypes of BIPOC.[17] To a large extent, this shift has been attributed to the replacement of older, less-tolerant whites by younger, more racially open-minded whites.[18]

However, as one looks more closely at the data, a more complicated picture emerges. In these same studies, whites lag far behind African Americans in supporting race-targeted policies and programs, such as affirmative action and government programs for minority businesses.[19] Instead of demonstrating less-overt racial prejudice than their elders, younger whites exhibit their racism in different ways. As opposed to overt derogatory actions and words, this "new racism" is characterized by racial apathy and colorblind racism. Racial apathy is simply not caring about racial inequality and choosing to avoid the issue altogether. This leads to aversive racism discussed later in this chapter. Colorblind racism (Chapter 7) denies the existence of racial differences altogether.

The more aggressive expression of overt racism can be seen in events like the 2017 white nationalist march in Charlottesville, Virginia. Events like that, Dylan Roof's murder of nine worshipers at Emmanuel AME church in Charleston, South Carolina, and clashes between the antifa and white nationalists in Portland, Oregon, give the impression that the number of virulent, organized racist and anti-immigrant whites is on the rise. Since the founding of the Ku Klux Klan in 1865, overt racism has had an organized voice in white nationalist groups. For the last several decades, their number of these groups had been declining. However, in recent years the Southern Poverty Law Center's database shows an increase, though it's unclear if more groups necessarily mean more white nationalist adherents.[20] With the election of President Donald Trump in 2016, these groups have become emboldened and the Internet has increased their visibility, giving them a broader public platform.[21] Nevertheless, the overall percentage of whites involved in such groups remains minuscule and doesn't represent the vast majority of white attitudes and actions toward BIPOC and immigrants. Even so, their presence indicates that overt racism is still something that must be confronted.

2. Backstage Racism

However, there are three other aspects of interpersonal racism that are often overlooked. The second form of interpersonal racism is how white people talk about BIPOC when they are with other white people. Researchers Leslie Picca and Joe Feagin refer to this as "backstage racism." They conducted a study of young adults who saw racism as largely a thing of the past while professing tolerance and commitment to racial equity. However, the researchers found that when these white young adults were in all-white groups, they made statements, used images, told jokes and related stories that were clearly and overtly racist. The researchers concluded that the purpose of this backstage racism was to create white racial solidarity and reinforce white superiority.[22]

After 11 years working in multiracial urban settings, my family and I moved to a small Midwestern town on the banks of the Mississippi. To my knowledge, in this town of approximately 25,000 people there was one Black man and one Jewish man who were year-round residents. Everyone else was white and saw these two families as different from them. Yet it was in this community that I heard more racially disparaging remarks than anywhere else I have lived. Young children and mature adults freely used the N-word and told racially charged stories and jokes they assumed were funny. I even heard a group of farmers blame their economic struggles on "Black girls having babies in the cities." Yet on the rare occasion when a person of color or a Jew came into their presence, they were as kind as could be. And when I took issue with their stories or remarks, they apologized for offending me, but I am sure they did not stop telling them when I was not around. That is backstage racism.

3. Aversive Racism

A third expression of interpersonal racism is what researchers Samuel Gaertner and John Dovidio call "aversive racism,"[23] which occurs when a white person's overt commitment to egalitarian values, including a denial of racial prejudice, conflicts with one's unconscious negative feelings toward—and beliefs about—racial minority groups. The negative feelings cause one to be uncomfortable, uneasy, fearful and even disgusted with BIPOC. Such beliefs and emotions result from subtle and explicit stereotypes absorbed in the person's upbringing and socialization. However, instead of becoming overtly hostile, the white person simply withdraws from the situation or relationship that gave rise to the uncomfortable feelings. Until the person is made aware of his avoidance behavior, he/she usually is not aware of this internal ambivalence.

4. Microaggressions

The final area of interpersonal racism is referred to as microaggressions, "the everyday verbal, nonverbal and environmental slights, snubs or insults, whether intentional or unintentional, which communicate hostile, derogatory or negative messages to target persons based solely upon their marginalized group [status]."[24] Often microaggressions are so subtle they can go unnoticed by other whites and leave BIPOC feeling uncomfortable without knowing exactly why. While not overt in-your-face expressions of hostility, they are clearly directed at one group over/against another. Richard Delgado and Jean Stefanic compare microaggressions to "water dripping on sandstone, [which] can be thought of as small acts of racism, consciously or unconsciously perpetuated, welling up from the assumptions about racial matters."[25] Microaggressions are generally the result of one's intrapersonal racism leaking out in barely perceptible ways. Whites usually need others to call their microaggressions to their attention, which can often result in white defensiveness and denial if one is not open to receive that kind of feedback.[26]

Microaggressions take many forms and can be directed at individuals because of race, gender or sexual orientation.[27] *Environmental microaggressions* are nonverbal cues in the arrangement, signage and/or language of a place that communicates some people are not wanted or should keep quiet. In an organization, if there are few BIPOC or women in positions of leadership, that can send the message that only white men are "qualified to lead." If spoken or assumed ground rules for a meeting exclude raising race-related issues, or there is a "commitment to colorblindness," BIPOC can feel silenced from sharing their deepest concerns.

Microassaults are conscious and intentional attitudes, beliefs and actions meant to demean or attack a person's racial identity, which can involve snide and subtle digs at a person, with labeling or words conveying underlying hostility. Microassaults often occur when a white person has a position of authority that gives freedom to do and say things; to challenge that behavior or language would jeopardize a BIPOC's livelihood or safety. Often microassaults are harbingers of more overt and discriminatory attitudes that lie just beneath the surface and come out under stress or strong emotion.[28]

Microinsults are rude and insensitive communications that demean a person's racial heritage or identity. Those who give microinsults are often unconscious that they are offering a snub. In fact, sometimes they may think they are offering a compliment. Statements like, "You are a credit to your race" or " You are not like others of your race" or "You speak such good English" betray an attitude that the speaker holds an overall low estimation of the person's racial group. When whites question whether a BIPOC got a job or received an award simply because of race, they betray a view that BIPOC are not capable and qualified.[29]

Microinvalidations are verbal and nonverbal communications that dismiss the ideas, feelings or experiences of BIPOC. When a Black person shares an experience of discrimination and is not taken seriously, when a Latinx couple are given poor service at a restaurant or when an Asian woman's ideas are coopted by others without giving her recognition, the target of such actions feels devalued. These are microinsults. Too often whites can talk about "valuing diversity," but their microinvalidations convey a contrary message.

Unlike overt racist actions and comments, microaggressions are subtle and often seem trivial when called out. However, whites need to realize that microaggressions are a daily experience for many BIPOC. Like drops of water slowly falling on the ground, over time microaggressions dig a deep hole in the souls of those who must contend with them at nearly every turn.[30] Over time, these constant challenges and assaults wear a person down, causing increased stress and damaged self-esteem. It's why BIPOC will sometimes say they have to work two-to-three times harder than their white counterparts to achieve the same recognition.

Institutional Racism

The third dimension of racism is *institutional racism*, which is embedded in the structure, policy and practices of an organization. Most of the established institutions of our society were founded at a time when racial equity and inclusion were not the norm or a major concern. Corporations, government agencies, hospitals, churches, nonprofits, universities and other such organizations came into being at a time when racial exclusion and division were the norm rather than the exception. Until the landmark 1954 Brown vs. Board of Education Supreme Court case, racial segregation was the law in most communities across the country. Thus these institutions were established to reinforce those disparities and enshrine them in their policies and practices, which became locked in and self-reinforcing to the degree that people in those institutions did not have to think or act in racist ways; the organization did it for them.[31] Because these practices are deeply embedded in organizational structure and culture, changing them can be extremely challenging and time consuming.

Numerous examples of institutional racism have come to light in recent years. The 2014 shooting of Michael Brown by Ferguson, Missouri, police officer Darin Wilson revealed how normalized the shooting of African Americans by white police officers had become in police districts around the country. Parents of children of color have begun to advocate for a more inclusive history curriculum in local schools and called attention to unfair disciplinary policies. Companies such as Denny's Restaurants[32] and Pepsi[33] had to face class-action lawsuits for engaging in racially discriminatory ways. Even in the example of Steven King that opened this chapter, one can easily see how institutional racism allowed the congressman to speak and act in racially discriminatory ways for his 16 years in Congress before he was censured.

Systemic Racism

Closely related to institutional racism is *systemic racism*, wherein the interrelationship of a network of institutions has incorporated racially discriminatory policies and practices over time that have become the accepted norm and practice. Legal scholar Michelle Alexander has called attention to systemic racism in the U.S. criminal-justice system and documented in exquisite detail the way in which young African American men have been treated in racially discriminatory ways from the time they are arrested to the way they are judged in the courts, from the length of their sentences to the severity of their jail terms and release from prison. Through the passage of laws in the War on Drugs during the Reagan administration and the adoption of stop-and-frisk and racial-profiling practices by police to sentencing guidelines in local courts, Alexander shows that the U.S. has instituted a "New Jim Crow Era" in the criminal-justice system.[34] Similar examples of systematized racism can be found in the housing and real-estate industry,[35] state education systems[36] and the practices of political parties,[37] to name just a few.

Daria Roithmayr, author of *Reproducing Racism*, illustrates this systemization process in housing segregation, explaining how in the mid-20th century in cities across the country, various institutions—including government agencies, banks, realtors and neighborhood associations—coordinated so as to exclude families of color from moving into certain neighborhoods. This process then locked in racial segregation in housing. She calls these arrangements "racial cartels," which over time normalize these practices and eventually are enforced without much thought or intention. Other institutions and systems like workplaces, schools and health facilities adjust their practices to accommodate the racial disparity. Eventually the system reaches a tipping point, where the ability to undo the racial disparity requires a complex, Herculean effort because people and institutions are highly invested in the status quo.[38] As in the case of institutional racism, systemic racism is self-reinforcing and becomes the standard practice by which everyone operates. Only when groups marginalized and oppressed by these systems begin to speak up and act in defiance of systemic practices does the embedded systemic racism begin to be challenged and changed.

The Fallacy of Saying One Is Not Racist

So often in conversations about racism, whites will defend themselves by claiming they are not racist. They don't use the N-word and don't support white nationalists. They try in every way to treat people equally and agree with Dr. King's charge to judge people by their character and not the color of their skin. In every way they seek to live a life in which racism is not evident or even tolerated.

The fallacy in this claim is that it assumes racism is only a personal belief or action and not woven through all aspects and levels of American life. Moreover, the claim of not being racist is a denial of one's participation in the systems and structures of society. Ibram X. Kendi, African American history professor and author of *How to Be an Antiracist*, takes the issue a step further when he writes, "The opposite of 'racist' isn't 'not racist.' It's 'antiracist.'" He continues:

> One endorses either the idea of a racial hierarchy as racist, or racial equality as an antiracist. One either believes problems are rooted in groups of people, as a racist, or locates the roots of problems in power and politics, as an antiracist. One either allows racial inequities to persevere, as a racist, or confronts racial inequities, as an antiracist. There is no in-between safe space of "not racist." The claim of "not racist" neutrality is a mask for racism.[39]

As long as whites remain complacent in their stance of not being racist, they remain part of a problem to be overcome. Racism is a cancer in our society. Either we work to overcome it or succumb to it.[40] There is no middle ground.

Conclusion

In the end, whites must come to terms with racism not just something we do or say, but something we are. We live in a society that was founded on openly racist principles (see more in Chapter 4 on "Facing Our Personal and National History") that are still operational today.[41] We exist in an institutional and systemic framework that continues to provide easier access to whites than BIPOC. While there may be individual exceptions, that doesn't alter the overall patterns. We live in a society that has blinded us to the ways in which whites receive benefits and privileges they did not ask for and many cases don't even know they have. Whites are allowed to ignore the vast array of data that indicates on almost every social scale—from education and health to job opportunities and criminal justice—that whites are favored consistently over BIPOC. We have a political system that grants the likes of Rep. Steven King a platform and power base with which to propagate his racially discriminatory views, until it becomes politically unfavorable.

As whites think about their race story and how racism has influenced their course and choices in life, they must think not only of the experiences they had witnessing overt racism, but also the way they avoided incidents when their race caused them problems and presented barriers to their options in life. They must think about the challenges they did not face and the barriers they did not have to overcome. They must think about the organizations they have been involved with—faith communities, employers and community groups—that excluded people who were not white or advantaged them because they were.

Racism in all its dimensions has raised and socialized whites and makes it difficult for many to see, much less accept, the realities of political, social and cultural racism at the heart of the American experience. This is the sea in which most people in the United States swim. And like fish who have no awareness of the water in which they live, so too whites in America are often unaware of the racist culture in which they live. Another name for this racist culture is "whiteness."

Whiteness and White Supremacy

Remember: all I'm offering is the truth, nothing more.
—Morpheus (The Matrix)

Racism as a White Problem

Shortly after World War II, author Richard Wright was asked by a French reporter to comment on the "Negro problem" in the United States. Wright responded by saying: "There isn't a Negro problem, only a white problem."[1] The reporter's question belies a common misperception among most white people regarding racism today. For many white people to talk about race is to talk about the plight and struggles of Black and Brown people and to respond appropriately. Or it's to defend the status quo against the various charges of injustice, unfairness and violence against BIPOC.

Following the shooting of Michael Brown in Ferguson, Missouri, the nascent hashtag #blacklivesmatter burst onto the scene as a national movement demanding Black and Brown bodies be given the same rights and protections as white people. Banners, signs, T-shirts, bumper stickers and the like with the words "Black Lives Matter" began to appear in communities across the country, especially where there was a plurality of BIPOC. Within a few weeks, counter-protestors emerged in predominantly white communities, asserting that "All Lives Matter" and "Blue Lives Matter," too. Instead of seeking to understand the fear of police violence that many Black and Brown people live under, most whites saw their cries as an assault on—and affront to—the "American way of life" in which they believed. While pointing the finger at angry and seemingly unruly BIPOC, whites failed to appreciate their own role in tragedies such as what occurred in Ferguson. They failed to see what Black people like Richard Wright had seen for decades, if not centuries: Racism is first and foremost a white problem.

It's also a problem that white people must address among themselves. Penn State professor Samuel Tanner points out that all too often when white people think and talk about racism, the conversation turns to what white people must do to right the wrongs committed against BIPOC.[2] If together with BIPOC, whites can figure out how to stop these injustices, then racism can be considered "solved." Tanner points out that there is a fatal flaw in this way of thinking because it assumes that racism is always and only about BIPOC. Moreover, white people feel like they can't really talk about or understand the dynamics of racism without being in conversation and concerted action with BIPOC. However, that is only half of the equation. Certainly, whites must learn to listen and validate the stories shared with them by BIPOC. Undoubtedly, they need to learn to share power and at times follow the lead of BIPOC. Unquestionably, they need to pay attention to their attitudes, microaggressions and unconscious biases. But at the same time, white people need to better understand themselves and the impact that whiteness has on them.

Tanner writes: "I'm convinced that white people also need to better understand white racial identity to engage in antiracism. I fear white supremacy is exacerbated when the problem of being white in a white supremacist society ... is not encountered."[3] In this chapter, we will do what Black feminist bell hooks[4] calls "interrogating whiteness," which she characterizes as "a persistent, rigorous and informed critique of whiteness."[5] First, we will explore the social construct of whiteness and its many qualities and expressions, including white privilege, the white racial frame, white cultural hegemony and whiteness as property. Then we will examine white supremacy as it is used today to describe the overarching power of whiteness in society.

The irony is that while whites, including even white academics, have not until recently made a serious study of what it means to be white in America, BIPOC have been studying white people for centuries. As bell hooks writes, "Although there has never been an official body in the United States ... gathered as anthropologists and/or ethnographers to study whiteness, Black people, from slavery on, shared in conversations with one another "special" knowledge of whiteness gleaned from close scrutiny of white people."[6] In 1920, W.E.B. Du Bois published an essay titled, "The Souls of White People,"[7] in which he analyzed and critiqued the myth of European superiority. For BIPOC, it was a matter of survival and safety to be able to decipher the ways and words of the white people around them and in positions of power. Now it's time for whites to catch up and realize, like Black and Brown people, that they have been racialized as white. This identity carries with it great privilege, but also precarious dangers that must be addressed.

White Socialization

When I was growing up in suburban Minneapolis in the 1960s, I knew that there was great upheaval taking place in communities across the southern United States and understood the issue to be a basic mistreatment of Black people in those communities. I knew there were marches taking place that often precipitated violence by whites who opposed the Blacks. I heard of the Ku Klux Klan and their violence against Blacks. But all of that seemed far away and unrelated to my life in overwhelmingly white Minnesota, where such problems (I thought) did not exist.[8] If someone had asked me about race, I might have talked about Black people or Native Americans. If someone had asked me what my race was, I would have responded that I did not have a race, that I was just an American. I would have answered in a way that most white people in the country at that time responded.

New York Times columnist Emily Bazelon writes: "Being white in America has long been treated, at least by white people, as too familiar to be of much interest. It's been the default identity, the cultural wallpaper." She goes on to point out that, in recent years, "White people are noticing something new: their own whiteness."[9] Because white people have not generally had to consider the impact of their whiteness on others and have not been socialized or educated to recognize the characteristics of whiteness, they have a great deal of catching up to do. Like me when I was younger, most white people consider their education, upbringing and ways of thinking and speaking to simply be the standard and norm for all people regardless of race. If white people are ever to be effective in talking with other whites about race-related issues, they need to understand the ways that whiteness controls their thinking and acting. In the vast majority of cases, any discussion of race almost automatically challenges what most white people consider to be normal and acceptable thought and behavior. Moreover, all people—especially those who are white—need to understand the impact that whiteness has and how it may tempt whites to soften or literally "whitewash" the hideous harm and injustice that racism has on BIPOC.

What Is Whiteness?

What do we mean by whiteness? Like the concept of race, whiteness is a social construct that has profound social, economic and political consequences in many parts of the world, and especially in the United States. According to Ruth Frankenberg,[10] whiteness is "a relational category" that has "content inasmuch as it generates norms, ways of understanding history, ways of thinking about self and others, and even ways of thinking about culture itself." Calling whiteness a "relational category" means that it sets the guidelines and norms for the way people of different racial and cultural groups should interact with one another. But because it's the dominant relational category, it can, has and still does determine those ground rules without input or even respect for the perspective of other racial and cultural groups it encounters. Whiteness rules. Richard Delgado and Jean Stefanic put it this way: "Whiteness is also normative—it sets the standard in dozens of situations" and has for several centuries in the U.S. and across much of the globe. Moreover, whiteness has historically been defined in contrast to those considered nonwhite and demarcated a line between those who had power and privilege and those who did not.[11] Thus whiteness came into being precisely when other people were categorized as a racialized other like Red, Brown or Black.[12]

However, as previously enslaved and colonized peoples have begun to assert their basic human rights, and in the United States as the percentage of whites compared to other racial groups continues to shrink, white people are becoming aware of their whiteness in profound and often troubling ways. Like the overall understanding of race and racism, whiteness continues to change and thereby challenge both whites and BIPOC in new ways. Defensive whites are thus correct when they say that the era of legalized segregation and slavery against BIPOC are a thing of the past, but are in error when they assume the powers of whiteness at work in a previous era are no longer operational in the present.

Frankenberg[13] describes whiteness as a series of "linked dimensions" that she identifies as "location of structural advantage often referred to as *white privilege*, a standpoint from which whites view themselves in what has been called a *racial frame* and a set of unrecognized and un-named *cultural practices*" [italics mine]. Harris[14] adds that, in a concrete way, whiteness operates as *property*. All of these in turn serve to shape a distinct white racial identity that one carries into the world at large. Let us look at each of these in turn.

White Privilege

When white people are confronted with the idea that they possess white privilege, they often get defensive and begin talking about how hard they have worked to get where they are in life. Many whites would agree with conservative commentator Ben Shapiro, who claims that white privilege is just a phrase designed to make white people feel guilty.[15] Its mention is often perceived as an accusation (as if the person stole something or got help they didn't deserve), when in reality it's a description of life in U.S. society. As Robin DiAngelo says: "Being white is a social and institution-al status ... imbued with legal, political, economic and social rights and privileges that are denied to others."[16] These privileges are illustrated by Peggy McIntosh, who listed 46 barriers or exclusions faced by African Americans not experienced by whites. They include such things as:

- I can if I wish arrange to be in the company of people of my own race most of the time.
- I can go shopping alone most of the time, pretty well assured that I won't be followed or harassed.
- I am never asked to speak for all people of my racial group.
- My culture gives me little fear about ignoring the perspectives and powers of people of other races.
- I can arrange to protect my children most of the time from people who might not like them.

- I can do well in a challenging situation without being called a credit to my race.
- Generally, I can be sure that if I ask to talk to the "person in charge," I will be facing a person of my own race.
- I can be sure that if I need legal or medical help, my race won't work against me.

McIntosh first created her list in 1989 and the circumstances have changed in the last 30 years, yet many of her examples, like those just listed, are still largely operational today. Her point is not that individual white people have done anything wrong, but simply to show these are "privileges" that whites can take for granted and many BIPOC cannot. Put another way, while white people face many challenges in life, they don't have to overcome those due to their race. These privileges are not due to one's educational level or economic status, but solely to the fact that one is considered racially to be white.

One of the limitations of the McIntosh list is that it focuses almost entirely on individual experiences and actions. Because whites tend to think of themselves in individual rather than collective terms, they can easily find examples in the list that have not been part of their personal experience. However, privilege operates largely through institutions and the wider culture of society that have been formed out of—and in conjunction with—whiteness and so are often invisible to those who have the privilege simply because they are not part of a white person's experience.

Stephanie Wildman[17] gives an example when she was called for jury duty. Each person in the prospective jury pool was asked a series of questions to determine his or her fitness to serve. In the beginning, each person was simply asked to introduce themselves. She noticed an Asian-looking man was asked, "Do you speak English?" The man grimaced when he answered that he did. Wildman observed that no other persons—except the Asian-looking people—were asked that question. Why? Because they had the "privilege" of not having to vouch for their ability to speak English. Did they do something untoward to avoid being asked that additional question? Of course not. That is how privilege works; it removes barriers others may face.

One of the key signs of privilege is that often success is characterized on the basis of merit and hard work, rather than built-in advantages. Moreover, when talking about whites and race, whites have a choice whether or not to join struggles against clear discrimination. Often when privilege is discussed, whites will insist that they have not said or done anything discriminating against persons or color, yet nor have they sought to challenge or confront other whites whose words or actions are clearly discriminatory. They have the freedom to remain silent. In his famous "Letter from Birmingham Jail," Dr. Martin Luther King, Jr., was most critical of those he called the "white moderate" who were not among those beating, hosing and jeering at Blacks, but remained silent and did not oppose those actions. They were more characterized by their inaction than any specific action.[18] This freedom to be silent and not act or speak up is a major privilege granted to white people precisely because they are not the targets of others' racial hatred.

Whether one is talking about education, the legal system, healthcare, beauty products and much more, whites find those systems and institutions readily serve their needs and interests; not so for BIPOC. While certain adjustments have recently been made to be more inclusive, such add-ons are exceptions to the dominant themes constructed and serving whiteness. Rather than seeing the mention of white privilege as an accusation, whites need to learn to how to critique the white racial frame through which they view and interact with others in their daily lives.

White Racial Frame

As Frankenberg stated above, in addition to privilege, whiteness is characterized by a distinct perspective whites have of themselves and others that goes largely unexamined.[19] Sociologist Joe Feagin refers to this as a white racial frame, the way whites have been socialized and educated to make meaning of race and racial differences. The racial frame is cognitive, emotional and behavioral, and helps explain why whites generally feel more comfortable in predominantly white social settings, lack any interest in challenging racism, feel defensive when they are referred to as privileged, and angry when they feel that race played a role in their being offered or denied an opportunity. The racial frame induces whites to trust the institutions and systems of society, such as education, law enforcement, finance, government, media and the military, and to feel betrayed when those institutions don't readily serve their needs.[20]

Feagin identifies two general characteristics of the white racial frame in contemporary life. The first is virtuous whiteness, which assumes that in any interracial interaction preference is given to whites over BIPOC. Whites are assumed to be operating out of virtuous intentions and thereby are entitled to a benefit of the doubt. White ways of being and thinking are regarded as normal and any suggestion of racism can be deflected, denied or minimized. The second dimension of the white racial frame is a negative stereotyping of BIPOC. Often the actions or words of BIPOC are seen as suspect, disrespectful and even harmful to the American way of life. Because of their nonwhite racial status, their concerns and needs are seen as secondary and even expendable. Depending on the racial group the "other" is identified with, they may be perceived as dangerous (African Americans), outsiders/intruders (Latinos), exceptionally smart (Asians), unpatriotic (Arab or Muslim) or primitive (Native Americans). Because of such depictions, which are continually reinforced by educational materials, media reports and the entertainment industry, the concerns of nonwhite groups are easily dismissed or ignored.[21]

A clear example of the white racial frame in operation can be seen in the outraged reaction by owners of the National Football League and many of their fans, when then-San Francisco 49ers quarterback Colin Kaepernick took a knee during the singing of the national anthem. While Kaepernick clearly stated that his action was meant to call attention to recent incidents of police brutality against African Americans, he was accused of being unpatriotic, dishonoring the flag and insulting members of the U.S. military. Kaepernick was vilified by fans, NFL owners and even the president of the United States. Ironically, in taking a knee Kaepernick was exercising his constitutional right to free speech, but that went largely unnoticed. The dominant white racial frames of many NFL fans and owners could not see or accept Kaepernick's action for what it was. By taking a knee, he challenged the integrity and veracity of law enforcement and the assumed virtue of white police officers. Moreover, he disrupted the freedom of white NFL fans to ignore the numerous incidences of police brutality against BIPOC. Because whites had not experienced this brutality, it challenged their sense what was considered normative in dealing with police or playing professional football. Moreover, Kaepernick himself was depicted as a spoiled athlete, an egotistical seeker of attention, a second-rate quarterback and ungrateful citizen. Even those NFL owners and other players who had sympathy for Kaepernick's action and position with it were pressured into silence for fear of losing their fan base and the vast revenues that came.[22]

The white racial frame is so "deeply internalized"[23] that most whites never question the attitudes, thoughts or emotions it can generate. Up until recently this white racial frame has gone largely unchallenged. However, in the aftermath of the death of George Floyd, BIPOC and their white allies have begun to challenge it. An example of this change is NFL Commissioner Roger Goodell's admission that he had been "wrong for not listening to players." While Goodell did not apologize to Kaepernick, he welcomed Kaepernick's return to the league and his input on how to better make decisions about players' rights to express their opinions.[24] He who was once vilified is now being welcomed. While only one example, this does foreshadow greater challenges to the white racial frames that may come in the future.

White Cultural Hegemony

In 2008, Barack Obama was elected as the 44th president of the United States, the first Black man to ever hold that office. Among some political progressives, Obama's election seemed to usher in a post-racial era when Dr. King's dream of being judged not by the color of one's skin but by the content of one's character had become a reality. However, for a large number of white Americans, Obama's ascendance to the highest political office ushered in what historian Richard Hughes calls "America's fourth time of trial" in which the nation faced a time of testing so severe that not only the form but even the existence of our nation [was being] called into question."[25] Encouraged by conservative politicians and funded by ideologically minded financiers like the Koch Brothers, there arose a movement called the Tea Party, whose expressed purpose was to oppose the policies and actions of the Obama Administration at every turn. The rallying cry of the Tea Party was "Take America Back." In 2016, it reached the pinnacle of its power in conjunction with the avowedly white nationalist alt-right movement and theologically conservative evangelical church leaders to bring about the election of Donald Trump as the country's 45th president. Trump's rallying cry had been "Make America Great Again."

While the rise of the Tea Party, the alt-right and Donald Trump all occurred in recent years, they represent what Richard Hughes calls the Myth of the Chosen Nation and the Myth of the Christian Nation, which explicitly see the United States as founded by and for white people under the guidance and blessing of the Christian God.

In calling to "Take America Back" and "Make America Great Again," this movement implicitly seeks to reinstate the United States as a nation for and governed by white people. In so doing, this movement illustrates what Ruth Frankenberg refers to as the third pillar of whiteness: a set of cultural practices that favor whites significantly over BIPOC.[26] While most whites would say that anyone can be an American, if one looks at U.S. history that is not true. What we see is that those groups deemed white have had a much easier time gaining full status and rights as citizens than those deemed nonwhite. As a result, white ways of thinking, acting and viewing the world have dominated throughout the nation's history.[27]

What it means to be an American largely derives from European cultures, particularly the countries of northern Europe and Great Britain. However, because of "the melting pot" myth, most Americans descended from Europe don't think of themselves as Europeans but as Americans.[28] Whatever culture one's white ancestors brought to the United States, they gave up to become American, which was in large part to be white. This process, referred to as assimilation, tends to take two to three generations and has often resulted in the loss of language, name changes and common cultural practices. While certain cultural customs around food or celebrations might remain, overall the culture of whiteness prevails. Thus the legal, educational and economic systems and all aspects of institutional life are derived from and shaped by what was culturally familiar and relevant to white Americans. At the heart of these systems was the idea that white ways were preferred and that whatever laws were passed or policies enacted were designed to benefit whites, or at least not significantly diminish their freedoms and opportunities. Thus laws and policies like affirmative action designed to correct past inequities against BIPOC have often been challenged as "reverse racism" because of the perceived disadvantage they represent to whites.[29]

When one looks at the distribution of wealth, elected officials, media executives, newscasters, teachers, college professors and the like, the vast majority of people in leadership positions are white.[30] The fact that people of African descent have been in North America for nearly 400 years and Barack Obama was the first and thus far only president of color exemplifies that disparity.

While the population of the U.S. represents many different subcultures, whites represent the dominant one, meaning that white ways of thinking, acting and being dominate. Other cultural groups must adjust and conform to white ways. For white people, their way of thinking and acting is the "right" way and the norm for interactions in daily life. While there may be individual deviations, to speak of culture is to speak of the dominant manner in which people and institutions are assumed to operate. Whether about history, morality, family structure, time orientation, decision-making or standards of beauty, the white preference and perspective dominates. And when individuals deviate from the preferred white ways, they are deemed irresponsible, deviant or antisocial.

The early 20th century sociologist W.E.B. Du Bois understood the dominance of white culture so clearly that he described African Americans experiencing what he called a "double-consciousness." Du Bois writes:

> It's a peculiar sensation, a double-consciousness, this sense of always looking at one's self through the eyes of others, of measuring one's soul by the tape of a world that looks on in amused contempt and pity. One ever feels his twoness—an American, a Negro; two souls, two thoughts, two unreconciled strivings, two warring ideals in one dark body, whose dogged strength alone keeps it from being torn asunder.[31]

Du Bois captures the essence of what it means to be part of a nation, but not accepted by the dominant white culture. While supposedly being American, African Americans in the early 1900s and even well into the 21st century feel their twoness and the cultural alienation Du Bois describes.

Sociologist Matthew Hughey calls this dominant white subculture "hegemonic." His use of the term "hegemony" derives from Italian Marxist Antonia Gramsci's[32] use of the word to describe the way in which an oppressive culture becomes so pervasive and dominant that it defines for those being oppressed what is normal, acceptable and possible. When hegemony is successful, Gramsci says that oppressed persons don't challenge it because they have come to believe that the status quo is fixed and unchangeable and, despite their suffering, they don't seek to challenge or liberate themselves from that oppression. Hughes says that hegemonic whiteness determines how nonwhites perceive themselves (identity) and the roles and obligations they are expected to fulfill. Hughey says: "From this perspective, hegemonic whiteness is neither essential nor innate, but appears 'natural' and 'common-sense.'"[33]

For whites, hegemonic whiteness manifests itself in two interrelated ways. First, whites perceive themselves to be different and superior to BIPOC. Second, they marginalize practices where individuals don't conform to expected white ways of thinking and acting.[34] For many whites, these hegemonic ways of being are largely unconscious. Whites are socialized into these ways of thinking and acting. Moreover, they are reinforced by school curricula, religious teaching, legal authority and political leaders. Whites are taught to fear ways that deviate from those prescribed and can suffer social, political and economic consequences for doing so.

I have experienced this pressure in my own life. As previously shared, I grew up in an exclusively white suburb of Minneapolis. If people in my community wanted to interact with BIPOC, we had to "go down" to the certain parts of the city; that phrase was a subliminal and subconscious message that we were going to some place lesser than where we lived. When I graduated from Duke University in 1975, I was hired to work as a youth worker in a low-income urban neighborhood that was demographically about one-third African American, one-third Puerto Rican and one-third white. On graduation eve, my father—who had financed my education—realized that I was going to go through with my plan to take the job. He had heard me say that was my desire many times, but I guess he assumed I would "come to my senses" when graduation arrived. However, two days before I was to graduate, he got angry with me for "throwing away my education," for which he reminded me that he had paid. Now, my father was reasonable, compassionate and a successful businessperson in a large corporation. He traveled the globe and was well respected in the business world. He had been successful in the white culture and expected me to do the same. He and my mother had raised my siblings and me to care for the "less fortunate" and to see ourselves as uniquely positioned to make a positive difference in the world. My actions deviated from the norms he had lived by and that he had sought to teach his children. In his mind, I was "wasting my education" because I had chosen to spend my energies working with racial "others" rather than the successful people (almost all white) who populated his world. I had broken the norms of the hegemonic culture that had served both my father and me well. He could not understand or accept my decision to go another way.[35]

As Hughey points out, the nature of the white dominant subculture has changed over the years. Many whites have become more open to other racial and ethnic groups than in the past. Moreover, recent protests have further challenged the norms of white cultural hegemony in ways not seen since the Rivil Rights Movement. In many cases, the experience I had with my father would not happen as much today. Yet there still remains a strong inclination among whites that social change, racial justice and cultural diversity are acceptable and perhaps even advantageous, as long as they don't diminish or undermine the dominance of white ways of being. As such, whiteness has become a form of property which must be protected and guarded from any attempt to steal or damage it.

Whiteness as Property

Legal scholar Cheryl Harris[36] tells the story of her grandmother, who in the 1930s participated in the great migration of Blacks who traveled to the North in search of better opportunities for their families, while fleeing the harsh discrimination of the Jim Crow South. While she had been a sharecropper, her "fair skin, straight hair and aquiline features" enabled her to "enter the white world ... not merely passing but trespassing" when she moved to Chicago. As a result, she was able to get a clerical job in a firm that "[catered] to the upper-middle class, understated tastes that required Blacks not be allowed." Every day she rode the bus from her predominantly Black neighborhood to the job, while hiding her racial identity and often enduring racist comments made in her presence "because of her presumed, shared [white] group affiliation." While Harris' grandmother worked that job for years without being found out, had she been discovered to be Black, she most certainly would have lost the job regardless of her accomplishments.[37] In reflecting on her grandmother's experience, Harris writes: "My grandmother's story illustrates the valorization of whiteness as treasured property in a society structured on racial caste."[38]

Beginning with the commodification of enslaved Africans as property, Harris documents how laws passed in the colonial period, the founding documents and various court cases throughout U.S. history demonstrate that "origins of property rights in the United States are rooted in racial domination."[39] As the slave trade and practice of slavery developed, slaves were bought and sold, traded for various goods and valued on the basis of their monetary worth.

Likewise, there was a parallel process whereby Europeans considered land occupied by Native American tribal groups as not having rights to their own land, thus it was deemed open to conquest with the removal of tribes from their land as justified. This process was aided by the fact that, to most indigenous groups, ownership of property was a foreign idea and so they willingly shared their land only to find themselves displaced and demeaned as not worthy of even residing on the land.[40] As Harris writes: "Although the Indians were the first occupants and possessors of the land of the New World, their racial and cultural otherness allowed this fact to be reinterpreted and ultimately erased as a basis for asserting right in land."[41]

By way of a thorough examination of case law, Harris shows how throughout U.S. history being considered white carried with it concrete social and economic benefits. Conversely, those same benefits were denied to Black and indigenous persons. Property in this sense did not just refer to tangible things, but also involved the right to work in certain jobs, pursue certain types of education and training, engage in otherwise restricted social relations, and access certain privileges and information. Well into the 20th century, being white carried legally protected advantages denied to Blacks and Native Americans.

Attempts to correct and compensate for these centuries-long inequities have been consistently challenged as unfair to whites. After the 1954 Brown vs. Board of Education case, which called for the desegregation of public schools, judges and legal scholars have taken a colorblind approach to the law.[42] Affirmative-action programs have come under scrutiny for being discriminatory against whites by making allowances for a certain number of guaranteed spaces for racial minorities. For instance, whites denied entrance to certain academic programs or jobs have claimed reverse discrimination against them as individuals, when the policies were designed to provide access to racially designated groups. Thus a person's whiteness was deemed a legal reason to claim discrimination.

However, beyond the law, if one looks at the disparities in income, education level, employment opportunities and promotions within organizations, there is a clear pattern of whites being favored out of proportion to their numbers in the population. Conversely, in terms of the criminal-justice system, whites are less often charged for similar crimes committed by Black and Brown people, and when convicted receive lighter sentences.[43] Thus, in all of these ways, whites are treated with a higher value than BIPOC.

Sociologist David Roediger has referred to this discrepancy as "the wages of whiteness."[44] In other words, there is a measurable financial advantage that comes with being white. Whether looking at inherited intergenerational wealth, family savings or pay levels for similar jobs, there is a pattern of whites as a group having a financial advantage over BIPOC. While there are individual exceptions, this pattern has held true for centuries.[45] Thus as Roediger says, it's entirely reasonable to see the interplay of race and economic status as something that historically and in the present benefits whites.[46]

Most whites are oblivious to what Cheryl Harris' grandmother experienced. By hiding her past as a Black sharecropper from Mississippi, she was able to access the rights and economic privileges that were denied her darker relatives and friends. She was assumed to possess whiteness and with it access to a world full of opportunities. While not as legally sanctioned as they once were, those advantages are still present in ways that BIPOC recognize, but whites often don't.

White Supremacy

In the 1989 film *The Matrix*, a computer hacker who goes by the name of Neo senses something wrong with the world and keeps encountering the word "matrix." Eventually he is led to a man named Morpheus, who explains the meaning of this word. Morpheus offers Neo a choice between taking a red or blue pill. The latter will return him to his former life oblivious of this Matrix he has encountered; the red by contrast will reveal to him the truth about the Matrix, a simulated reality in which individuals are controlled by forces beyond their awareness and yet dictate every aspect of their lives. Neo chooses the red pill and instantly finds himself engaged with forces that seek to keep him blind or kill him for his awareness. However, once Neo sees the world for what it is, he cannot go back to his former blind ignorance and so engages in a protracted battle against the forces that would blind him.[47]

Once whites begin to perceive the pervasive influence that whiteness has over their daily lives, it's not unlike Neo choosing the red pill. Situations and experiences that simply seem benign become deeply troubling. Long-held beliefs about American history and the adventurous spirit that created the country is reframed into a story of horrifying genocide and unrelenting oppression. Things taken for granted are now seen as the product of generations of privileged status and access. And the great American story of prosperity is recognized to have been achieved on the backs of unwilling slaves and stolen indigenous land. While the positive myths that shaped our national self-identity need not be totally

rejected, the other side of the story paints a much fuller, if more complicated picture.

According to historian Richard Hughes,[48] "The Myth of White Supremacy" is the foundational but largely unacknowledged myth that defines
and undergirds the American story. He writes that it "stands at the heart
of the nation's self-understanding ... like the air we breathe, surrounding us, enveloping us and shaping us, but in ways we seldom discern."[49]
By myth, Hughes doesn't refer to some fanciful but fictional story. He
defines it as "a story that, whether true or false, helps us discern the
meaning and purpose of our lives and, for that reason, speaks truth to
those who embrace it."[50] When speaking of American history, Hughes
says myths "are stories shared in common by the American people—or
at least by the majority of Americans—stories that convey, reinforce and
help us affirm commonly shared convictions regarding the purposes and
meaning of the nation."[51] Myths are the building blocks of our culture,
systems of government and education, and other institutional systems of
our society. At the heart of all of these is white supremacy.

Now when individuals encounter the world of white supremacy, they often think of the KKK or outspoken white nationalists like David Duke
or the horrific stories of lynchings and cross burnings of the 19th and
20th centuries. That is *not* how I am using the phrase. Rather, at its most
basic level, white supremacy is "an ideology of the inherent superiority
of white Europeans over nonwhites, an ideology used to justify crimes
against indigenous peoples and Africans that created the nation ...
that rationalizes racial disparities in wealth and well-being and justifies
whites, particularly white men disproportionately occupying leadership
positions in the most powerful institutions in society."[52]

Like *The Matrix*, white supremacy operates without being named and
recognized unless one knows how to look for the signs. It operates
through media representations that shape what one sees as good or bad,
right or wrong, important or insignificant. It operates through laws and
policies that govern everyday American life. It shapes the practices of institutions and defines what constitutes success. While in past eras white
supremacy was often quite explicit in how it governed the attitudes and

behaviors of whites and BIPOC, in our current era it often operates by what is omitted, ignored or trivialized.

For several years, I taught a graduate course—Race and Ethnic Relations—in which I had my students read *A Different Mirror* by Ronald Takaki, a former professor of Ethnic Studies at Stanford University who relates the histories of various ethnic groups making up the fabric of American society. My students read about the histories of African slaves and Native Americans, as well as those of Russian Jews, Mexicans, Filipinos, Chinese, Japanese, Irish and Middle Easterners. All of these ethnic groups in their own way had to contend with the discrimination and oppression that came from white supremacy. When they were done with the book, a common question was: *Why had we not been exposed to these histories in our earlier courses on U.S. history?* The central role of white supremacy was never part of their study and so those histories were ignored and omitted.

In terms of the systems and institutions that govern society, the impact of white supremacy is clearly evident. Public school systems with a greater percentage of students of color are regularly less funded by state governments than those with a greater percentage of whites.[53] Average wealth and income statistics consistently show Black and Brown families lagging behind white families in basic family incomes.[54] In the criminal-justice system, Black and Brown defendants are routinely convicted more often and punished more severely than their white counterparts committing the same crimes.[55] And while the statistics on these and other issues are easily accessible in the public sphere, little seems to change because the goal of white supremacy is to keep whites in an overall position of power and privilege.

By extension, white supremacy creates a culture that highlights individualism, meritocracy and perfectionism. As a result, any attempt to draw attention to the kinds of disparities mentioned above are dismissed as being due to hard work on the part of the winners and laziness on the part of the losers. Any attempt to see the issues through a racial frame or acknowledging white privilege creates defensiveness and anger, and is often dismissed. When the subject of race and racism comes up, white supremacy has conditioned whites to be defensive and deny the evidence of disparity and marginalization. Moreover, it has taught them to flee the discomfort the topic of race often creates and withdraw or avoid conflict at all cost, rather than face the truth of the situation. While some allowances and changes may be made to address inequities, they are always done in a way that allows whites to remain the dominant racial group overall.

In a real sense, white supremacy is another name for systemic racism; however, as Edgar Villanueva points out, using the term white supremacy "explicitly names who in the system benefits and—implicitly—who bears the burdens."[56] The term "white supremacy" looks at systemic racism through the lens of how whites benefit unjustly in a society that claims "liberty and justice for all."

Invited to the Journey and the Struggle

This chapter explains in detail the characteristics and processes of whiteness and white supremacy: the sea in which all Americans—white, African American, Latino, Asian American, Native American and immigrant—swim. Too often, well-meaning whites seeking to be allies for racial justice fail to realize that overcoming racism and white supremacy is more than just finding ways to get along. Certainly, in this regard, we as a nation—in spite of our recent polarities—are much further along than generations before us. Yet the disparities discussed in this chapter continue to exist. Even in the effort to become aware of racism within themselves and the world around them, most Americans are still impacted by the power and "logic" of white supremacy. Moreover, the white people in our lives with whom we want to have conversations about race are immersed in this culture just as we are.

In constructing and reflecting on our race story, like Neo, whites must be willing to face the difficulty and discomfort of going against the grain of white supremacy at the foundation of our culture. They must concur with Richard Wright that racism is a white problem and, while whites must work with their colleagues and friends of color, there is a great deal of work that needs to be done white person to white person. Seeking to encourage other white people to enter the discomfort of examining their implicit biases, conscious and unconscious racism, and the way their lives have been shaped by white supremacy means that they too must face that discomfort and struggle. We invite others into a journey, a pilgrimage of sorts, on which we ourselves have embarked.

While this journey is difficult and uncomfortable, recent research has revealed that while racism and white supremacy negatively impact BIPOC, they also hurt and cripple white people as well. It's to that subject we turn in the next chapter.

How Racism Hurts White People

The wound is there and it's a profound disorder,
as great a damage in his mind as it's in his society.
—Wendell Berry

Racism as Mental Illness

Thus far I have focused largely on the damage that racism and white supremacy have caused BIPOC throughout history and in the present; however, racism has not and does not only hurt BIPOC; racism also has disintegrating and damaging effects on white people.

Wendell Berry puts it this way:

> If white people have suffered less obviously from racism than black people, they have nevertheless suffered greatly; the cost has been greater perhaps than we can yet know. If the white man has inflicted the wound of racism upon black men, the cost has been that he would receive the mirror image of that wound into himself....The wound is there and it's a profound disorder, as great a damage in his mind as it's in his society.[1]

The nature of this defect in whites was first introduced to me by the late Dr. James Tillman, who wrote: "The refusal of whites to acknowledge and discuss white racism is caused by insecurity and an unhealthy self-love" and is a sign of collective mental illness in which "the consistent use of race as the central and ultimate criterion by which the white man in Western Culture judges non-white people and therefore himself."[2] The use of race in this way "produces in the white personality a *defect* which is *expected* in and *patterned* by, our culture. This irrationality in matters of race ... is a *normal* part of our culture."[3] In other words, racism distorts and cripples the character of white individuals, but that distortion

becomes normalized (and therefore made acceptable) in white supremacist culture.

Historical Intergenerational Racial Trauma

James Tillman was a sociologist and not a psychiatrist, and wrote those
words before recent discoveries in neuroscience. However, in the last
decade what Tillman described has now been further validated by recent
findings in neuroscience about the nature, causes and effects of historic
trauma. Psychiatrists have long known the experience of trauma is clearly related to violent and tragic life events, like natural disasters, participation in war, physical and sexual abuse, and other forms of violence.
What has come to light more recently is how the impact of trauma, if not
properly addressed, can be transferred intergenerationally, which may
occur as dysfunctional behavior and thought patterns modeled by the
parent and then picked up by the child. Even more significantly is how
trauma can actually alter a parent's DNA so that the impact of that trauma
is transferred at the genetic level. This discovery has led to a recognition
of what is now referred to as historical trauma.[4]

Reesma Menakem, an expert on somatic trauma, writes: "Historical
trauma has been likened to a bomb going off, over and over and over
again."[5] In its simplest form, trauma is the human body's natural defensive response to minimize or stop something perceived as dangerous to
it. If a person or community experiences repeated negative occurrenc-
es, the response gets embedded and stuck in the body, and becomes a
handicap rather than a protection. The whole process we call trauma occurs at a subconscious and physical level, activated by the reptilian brain
where the automatic fight-flight-freeze response originates its automatic
responses to real and perceived threats. Only after the reaction does the
cognitive brain catch up to try explaining the subconscious automatic
response. Repeated over and over among people of a particular population, that trauma response becomes part of the culture and norms of a
people.

Dr. Joy DeGruy was the first writer to apply the insights of historical
trauma to the experience of racism. Having reviewed the 400-year history of enslavement, lynchings, marginalization, police brutality and

other forms of physical, social, psychological and institutional violence, she suggests that—as a collective—Black people in America must grapple with what she calls Post-Traumatic Slave Syndrome (PTSS), "a condition that exists when a population has experienced multigenerational trauma resulting from centuries of slavery and continues to experience oppression and institutionalized racism today. Added to this condition is a belief (real or imagined) that the benefits of the society in which they live are not accessible to them."[6] Following DeGruy's lead, therapists like Menakem have developed therapeutic interventions to help individuals, families and whole communities find ways to heal from the effects of this intergenerational trauma.[7]

Similar studies have identified historical trauma among Native Americans. For over 500 years, they have experienced the loss of native lands, destruction of culture, separation of families through the Indian schools, and brutal and systemic violence designed to eliminate them. The population of indigenous peoples in North America has decreased by 95% since the time of Columbus in 1492. The result has been higher than average rates of domestic violence, alcoholism, drug abuse and suicide among Native American populations. Life expectancy for Native Americans is 2.4 years less than all U.S. populations and contributes to higher rates of heart disease, tuberculosis, STDs and diabetes than any other racial/ethnic group in the U.S.[8]

Historical trauma has been documented in a variety of populations, such as Holocaust survivors, descendants of those held in Japanese-American internment camps and victims of the Khmer Rouge violence in Cambodia. While there are many common characteristics like depression, anxiety, suicidal thoughts, abuse, violence and victim identity, each group and context has its own unique features and different means of developing resilience in the aftermath of traumatic events.[9] Mental-health professionals and neuroscientists now recognize that historical intergenerational trauma can have a long-term effect on families, communities and nations.

The Impact of Trauma on Whites

Given what is known of the history of slavery, genocide, violence and oppression against communities of color in this country, DeGruy's and others' insights on historical trauma are significant. However, what has been largely unnoticed and subjected to cultural denial is the impact of that same history on the descendants of the oppressors: the impact of historical trauma on white people. In his study of the impact of the Holocaust on the German national identity, Bernard Giesen[10] noted that the impact of racism on the perpetrators has been largely overlooked. While racism has caused deep and extensive suffering on its victims, it also has brought about a loss of humanity on the part of perpetrators, the unknowing historic beneficiaries of that racism. In propagating, justifying and then minimizing the history of racism, white people have lost contact with their integrity and basic morality.[11] Speaking more directly to the experience of white Americans, Native American scholar Mark Charles states that "it's impossible to be complicit with centuries of traumatizing oppression without becoming traumatized oneself."[12]

Menakem refers to the historical trauma impacting both BIPOC and white people as white-body supremacy trauma. He writes:

> For the past three decades, we've earnestly tried to address white body supremacy in America with reason, principles and ideas—using dialogues, forums, discussions, education and mental training.... But we've focused our efforts in the wrong direction. We've tried to teach our brains to think better about race. But white-body supremacy doesn't live in our thinking brains. It lives in our bodies.[13]

After building on DeGruy's work on the impact of PTSS on Black people in America, Menakem turns his attention to the impact of white-body supremacy on white people.

While white-body supremacy trauma made its impact on people of African descent and Native Americans beginning around the 1600s, the impact of this trauma on white people starts several hundred years earlier during an age of countless wars and brutality. Executions, torture and Coliseum battles were community events where if one were not a victim of violence, one was a spectator. The most powerful and brutal purveyor of this violence was the nation of England, the dominant power in Europe and in the

American colonies. The first Europeans to settle en masse in North America were Puritans and Pilgrims fleeing persecution and imprisonment for their religious beliefs. Nancy Isenberg[14] notes that the vast majority of white indentured servants who were brought to Jamestown, Virginia, were destitute people scooped off the streets of London or pulled out of overcrowded prisons. The newly "discovered" North America became an easy receptacle for England's unwanted and neglected people.

Reflecting on England's brutality and its traumatic impact on the first European arrivals to the United States, Menakem asks: "Isn't it likely that many of them were traumatized by the time they arrived here?" Answering his own question, he writes: "When the English came to America, they brought much of their resilience, much of their brutality and I believe, a great deal of their trauma with them."[15] Seen through the lens of historic trauma, the rigid brutality of the Puritans against those who violated their codes makes sense, as does their vicious dehumanization of the indigenous and African peoples. Likewise, the British persecution of the Irish helps to explain the brutal violence of the Irish against Black people in cities like New York and Philadelphia when they arrived in North America.[16] Moreover, the institutions of slavery and the inhuman buying and selling of human bodies, make sense in light of historical trauma. As the saying goes: "Hurt people hurt people." Traumatized whites turned their pain toward those more vulnerable than themselves, which in turn institutionalized white supremacy in the nation's political, economic and cultural life of the nation.

White Fragility

The clearest indication of the effects of white supremacy body trauma is what Robin DiAngelo calls white fragility.[17] She describes it this way:

> White Fragility is a state in which even a minimum of racial stress becomes intolerable, triggering a range of defensive moves. These moves include the outward display of emotions, such as anger, fear and guilt, and behaviors such as argumentation, silence and leaving the stress-inducing situation.... This insulated environment of racial privilege builds white expectations for racial comfort while at the same time lowering the ability to tolerate racial stress.[18]

This definition makes evident three key points. First, because of the historical trauma experienced by BIPOC and white people, cross-racial interactions or even the topic of race in homogeneous settings can be inherently stressful. Second, in accordance with the nature of trauma, the defensive reactions of whites to the reality of race is automatic, triggered by the reptilian brain[19] and not a function of conscious rational thought. Third, the discomfort caused by white fragility functions as a means of protecting the racial privilege whites possess by insulating or removing them from the uncomfortable situation caused by racial stress. Menakem identifies what he calls "the fantasy of white fragility" that "Black bodies are incredibly strong and frightening and impervious to pain." By contrast "white bodies are extremely weak and vulnerable, especially to Black bodies. So it's the job of Black bodies to care for white bodies, soothe them and protect them."[20] Menakem goes on: "The myth [of white fragility] has been reinforced by a second fantasy.... Because white bodies are so vulnerable to Black ones, when a Black body is not subservient to a white one, it must be brutalized or destroyed" ... so as to keep the white body safe. On a cognitive level none of this make sense; rather, these fears and brutal responses lie in the body, which in turn is connected to the reptilian brain and its fight/flight/freeze response.[21]

Menakem contends that the myth of white fragility gave whites a justification maintaining oppressive power over Black people; they saw it as essential to their well-being. Today while whites have done away with the overt structures of racial oppression, their fear of Black bodies continues. In the presence of BIPOC, particularly Black people, whites can experience feelings of fear, discomfort, defensiveness and anger for no apparent reason. While whites may use any number of rationalizations for their responses (which Menakem lists), the reality is that in those encounters whites are experiencing secondary trauma.[22]

Most whites today might deny the white fragility fantasy that Menakem describes. Yet they are hard-pressed to explain their automatic responses of fear and insecurity when they are in situations where they are a racial minority, and the deep sigh of relief experienced when they are warmly welcomed by BIPOC. As a manifestation of trauma, these reactions don't originate on a conscious level, but of the reptilian brain where trauma resides.

The evidence of white fragility expresses itself in a multitude of forms. When white people have their assumptions or behaviors challenged, they experience a variety of emotions such as being singled out, attacked, silenced, shamed, accused or judged. They may express those feelings by crying, physical and emotional withdrawal, arguing, denial or seeking absolution. Often when confronted by the racist nature of their words or actions, whites will defend themselves by referencing their intentions rather than owning the impact of those words or actions. They will offer a range of defensive rationalizations, such as claiming to have friends of color, dismissing the observation as just the speaker's opinion, accusing the speaker of "playing the race card," charging reverse racism, expressing feelings of being hurt, claiming innocence and much more. A common reaction is seeking to rationally explain words or actions, citing studies and statistics and in other ways avoiding responsibility for the emotional impact of what has been said and done. Another common response is to go to the other extreme and express white shame and guilt, as if the confession without a clear change of behavior should lead to absolution.

White fragility serves many functions that reinforce whites' privileged status. Some of those include closing off any self-reflection by whites, silencing the discussion, making whites feel like they are victims of BIPOC's anger or demands, and keeping whites from dealing with the reality of racism in a given situation. Feeling like victims of others' prejudice, whites may seek solidarity and vindication from other whites for their thoughts or feelings, thus undermining constructive feedback. Whites will try to make the conversation about something other than race, like one's personality or class or the context of the discussion. In essence, white fragility seeks to derail or dismiss any instance where a white person receives feedback on actions or words that have been identified as racist. To call out another is to be unfair or emotional or just out of line.

When talking with white people about issues of race, a person should expect to encounter these and many other expressions of white fragility. Those who are white should be cognizant of the same emotional and behavioral reactions in themselves. BIPOC may experience a feeling of disgust with what they consider typical white behaviors or conversely a desire to soothe the white person in his or her discomfort.[23] The purpose in pointing out white fragility is not to belittle or condemn, but to recognize it as a natural response to centuries of white-body supremacy trauma, and to help white people move past the dysfunctional response that white fragility evokes to a more engaged and constructive form of interaction.

At the same time, it's important to realize that because white fragility is a mechanism to maintain a white person's privileged social and racial status, overcoming white fragility can be a painful and arduous process. Whenever I have conducted classes or courses on racism, I let students know that engaging with racial issues is inherently uncomfortable in U.S. culture. I predict (with a high degree of accuracy) that whites will feel defensiveness, guilt and being overwhelmed, and that BIPOC will experience anger, frustration and despair. Having laid out this path, I then invite them to courage, which I define as moving forward in the face of fear. In my view, there is no other option if we are to come to grips with the historic racial trauma that afflicts whites as a group.

Dying of Whiteness

Dr. Jonathan Metzl[24] is a physician who has taken the discussion of racism's impact on white people a step further. Through numerous interviews with middle- and low-income whites, Metzl explores how whites often vote for politicians who support policies that work against their own health and well-being. They have been led to believe by conservative politicians that government programs supporting healthcare, strengthening gun laws, supporting quality public education and other such programs are not in their self-interest. Such programs have been characterized as benefiting BIPOC and immigrants, even though far more whites than BIPOC benefit from those programs. Metzl notes that such policies are presented in racially coded terms, creating 'white backlash politics' that often hurt middle- and low-income whites as much as they hurt BIPOC. In so doing, these white people are allowing their overt or covert racist perspectives to undermine their own physical well-being. As Metzl says, such people are "dying of whiteness."

By whiteness, I am not referring to individual racist attitudes or actions, but rather the systemic racism discussed in Chapter 3: about laws and policies that either threaten people's livelihood, like state decisions to limit expansions of the Affordable Care Act or opportunities for advancement, such as in states cutting back on public-education funding. While such laws and policies have a negative effect on the health and livelihood of BIPOC, they also negatively impact middle- and low-income white people. Such white supremacist actions are designed to advance white privilege and keep BIPOC "in their place," negatively impacting whites as well.

Recognizing the Need for Healing

Tillman[25] referred to racism as a mental-health issue from which we must be healed as individuals, as people groups and as a nation. Menakem identifies the ways in which whites experience secondary trauma in relation to Black people. He invites them to become more aware of their bodily reactions as a way of countering their experience of white fragility.[26] Meanwhile, conservative politics that play to those basic fears hurt the very people they are supposed to help: middle- and low-income whites. Metzl points out that changing people's political views is difficult. Before we can invite our white friends and colleagues to engage in these and other therapeutic processes, we need to help them see that they are debilitated by their historic racial trauma inherited by previous generations and modeled by white parental and authority figures. As Stephen Covey has so aptly said in another context, "How we see the problem is the problem."[27] If whites continue to see BIPOC as threatening, and calls for structural and systemic change as asking for too much, then they remain blind to their own fragility and disability. However, if they can be helped to see their reactions to BIPOC and issues of race as a sign of their own dysfunctional white fragility, then steps toward racial justice and healthy interracial interaction can begin. Understanding the impact of white-supremacy body trauma, white fragility and white-supremacist politics can also give us empathy for the difficult challenge that white people face in their own racism and its debilitating effects. That empathy need not cause us to be soft in speaking the truth about racism's socially unjust and personally devastating consequences for BIPOC, but can give us patience with the process that all whites must go through toward a more antiracist perspective and lifestyle.

Knowing Our Histories

The past is never dead. It's not even past.
—William Faulkner

Slaves Built the White House

On July 25, 2016, Michelle Obama delivered a stirring speech at the Democratic National Convention in Philadelphia to offer her support to Hillary Clinton's candidacy for U.S president. The overall point of her speech was to say that Clinton could and should be the first woman to assume the presidency. In the midst of making that point, she reflected on the fact that her husband had been the first Black man to be elected president and spoke these words: "I wake up every morning in a house that was built by slaves." Her point was that we as a nation have moved past that barrier and could move past others.[1]

The crowd in the hall that night gave her a standing ovation. However, as often happens in a racist society infused with white supremacy, Obama's statement was taken out of context and misconstrued. The next day, media pundits reacted to the stark honesty of her statement. The progressive press generally applauded her, but many conservatives took umbrage.

One commentator said that Obama "stretched the truth"[2] because there have been many renovations since the first building of the White House. Another insisted that the government paid the slaves. Another said that whites also worked on the White House. And Fox commentator Bill O'Reilly said that while they were slaves, they were "well-fed." Fact checkers affirmed that there were others besides slaves who helped built the White House, but the slaves were not paid; their masters were. Only one free Black, Philip Reid, was paid directly.[3] Well-fed or not, they were still people in bondage to their white master.[4]

This extreme overreaction to Obama's speech betrays our culture's discomfort with the nation's history of racism, slavery and white supremacy. Not only do most people of all races not know our nation's history, what they do know or think they know is often highly distorted. Obama's assertion that slaves helped build the White House is not an item of historical controversy. Likewise, slavery happened. The Fugitive Slave Law was the law of the land. Jim Crow, Black codes, lynchings, children being attacked by dogs and horses in Birmingham, Native American children separated from their families, Japanese internment camps, the assassinations of Medgar Evers, Martin Luther King, Jr., and other activists are established facts in our history. And yet so often white people want to ignore or minimize those facts as if they have no bearing on our present situation.

Understanding our nation's history is crucial because it shapes the way we understand and interpret our personal histories with race and racism. When the topic of racism in U.S. history is broached, many whites will often insist they were not alive at the time and so they should not be held accountable for past actions. And yet who and where we are today is a product of that history and, if we are ever going to talk openly and honestly about the impact of racism in our systems, institutions, culture and individual lives, we must be aware of the history of racism in our country.

Furthermore, it's important for anyone attempting to interact with white people about racism in our country to be aware of the ways in which they have been impacted by that history. More importantly, in honesty and humility, we must be open about how we ourselves are also continually impacted by that history. As Elsie in Dominique Morisseau's brilliant play *Mud Row* says: "We remember our history so we know where we are and so we can get to somewhere else."[5]

The Filter of the Master Narrative

Most white people in the United States have a limited understanding of the history of racism in their country, and its impact on the shape and direction of their lives. What little most people know comes from the inadequate exposure they are given in the educational system. Moreover, the atrocities and horrors experienced by BIPOC, starting with the near genocide of the indigenous peoples already residing here, is highly sanitized. National holidays like Independence Day, Columbus Day and Martin Luther King Jr. Day have been drained of the brutality experienced by BIPOC in our history. Thus, it's not surprising that most whites are overwhelmed when confronted the full story of racial brutality.

Historian Ronald Takaki[6] has pointed out that what most people know of U.S. history is based on what he calls "the Master Narrative of American History," which has served as a filter to construct an account that places European immigrants and their achievements at the center of the story. While people from all over the world have migrated to this country, it was only the European migrants whose story got highlighted. What history is recorded of other racial/ethnic groups has been treated as subsections to the main story of whites moving westward to claim and settle the western frontier. Because this Master Narrative has been shaped by the previously discussed Myth of White Supremacy, the historical experiences of non-European peoples has been minimized or altogether omitted. Thus most Americans, particularly white Americans, have not been exposed to the racist horrors of America's past. Many whites don't know what they don't know.[7]

Key Markers in the History of Racism and White Supremacy

Racism in Many Forms

So what are some of the key markers in the history of racism and white supremacy in U.S. history? First, it is important to note that racism has and continues to take many forms. For starters, there is the history of settler colonialism toward the indigenous peoples living in North America when the first Europeans began to migrate in large numbers. This settler colonialism led to the displacement of the indigenous peoples from their native lands, resulting in a level of genocide that nearly or totally eradicated whole people groups. Scholars estimate that in 1492 there were somewhere between 10 and 18 million indigenous people living in the area of the continental United States; today that number is estimated to be five million.[8] It's a history of treaties made and repeatedly broken by the white leaders, a pattern that continues to this day as the government repeatedly ignores treaties granting Native American tribes sole ownership of land and opens them for mining, lumber and other corporate interests.[9]

The second expression of racism in our history involves the mass capture, transfer and enslavement of peoples from West Africa and the long history of violence toward, discrimination against and marginalization of African Americans. For over 200 years, Africans were the property of white masters who bought, sold and used them as property. This practice led to the Civil War, which ultimately gave Blacks full citizenship on paper, but not in the actual application of law. Thus an effort to fully realize their constitutional rights has been ongoing from 1865 until the present.[10]

The third and perhaps least known is the marginalization and fixed second-class status of peoples of non-European origins in addition to Native Americans and African Americans. In this stream are the people who went from being Mexicans to being second-class Americans because of treaties and wars that led to the U.S. annexation of lands formerly under Mexican rule. It also includes people from Asia—Chinese, Japanese and Filipino—specifically imported to work the fields and build railroads in the western part of the country. It includes the native peoples of Hawaii and Alaska, whose culture and livelihoods were subsumed under American corporate and military interests. Each of these groups and more were not granted citizenship without a protracted struggle, even though their contribution to the growth and development of the nation was essential.[11]

Like the many-headed Hydra of ancient Greek mythology,[12] racism has been expressed and lived out in history in many forms. And like that mythical creature, even when it seems that racism in one form has been addressed or at least pushed back, history has shown that racism has come back in another form. In addition to being given a sense of the context that racism's history has created, we must realize that racism continues to re-emerge in new ways and hideous expressions.

White Supremacy from the Beginning

On the 76th anniversary of the signing of the Declaration of Independence, on July 5, 1852, the African American abolitionist Frederick

Douglass spoke in Rochester, New York. The title of his speech was, "What to the Slave Is the 4ᵗʰ of July?" He eloquently pointed out that the freedoms enshrined in the Declaration of Independence and later the Constitution were intended only for those of European descent.[13] In fact, those founding documents clearly stated that non-Europeans were less than fully human.

The Declaration of Independence begins its second paragraph with the words: "We hold these truths to be self-evident, that all men are created equal, that are endowed by their Creator with certain unalienable rights, that among these are Life, Liberty and the pursuit of Happiness." However, going further down the page from those illustrious words, one reads about "the merciless Indian savages whose known rule of warfare is undistinguished destruction of all ages, sexes and conditions."[14] Not only do those words refer to indigenous peoples in the basest of terms, but also the actions they describe are the very behaviors the European colonists *enacted against them.* In this founding document, Native Americans are excluded from the human beings who are "created equal," and are confined to a category that makes them scarcely human at all.

Native Americans are not mentioned in the Constitution, but enslaved Africans are (although the word "slave" is not actually used). There we find what is called the "Three-Fifths Clause." For the purposes of determining the number of people for representation in Congress, enslaved Blacks were considered to be three-fifths of a person. The southern states wanted to keep slavery legal, but did not want to give those slaves any rights as citizens. In order to save the fragile union of the newly founded United States, representatives of the non-slaveholding states agreed to count slaves as three-fifths of a person for the purpose of the census. While some would argue that this did not mean they considered slaves as such, in effect that is what it implies.[15] In reality, enslaved Africans had no rights by law and were routinely denied the same rights as white people when it came to the courts. Moreover, well into the 20ᵗʰ century, laws were in place that made it difficult, if not impossible, to exercise the most basic of rights, including voting, marrying the person of choice regardless of race, and living in whatever neighborhood they chose. Whatever the original rationale, the three-fifths clause enshrined in law and practice betrays a conviction that African Americans were—and sometimes are still—not treated as full citizens.

For people of all other races and ethnicities, there have been a series of laws passed in U.S. history expressly designed to limit the citizenship of people not originally considered to be white, such as Irish or Italians. The sources of many of these laws were the naturalization acts of 1790, 1798 and 1802. Each of these bills limited the right of naturalized citizenship to "free white persons of good character." Excluded from citizenship were Native Americans, indentured (white) servants, Black slaves, free Blacks and later Asians.[16] Specific laws were eventually passed to restrict the rights of ethnic groups such as The Indian Removal Act (1830), The Treaty of Guadalupe Hildago (1848),[17] The Chinese Exclusion Act (1882), The Filipino Repatriation Act (1935) and the forced incarceration of all Japanese-Americans (1942).[18]

While not technically a U.S. law, another founding document that has shaped American law is a 15th-century Papal bill called the Doctrine of Discovery. In essence, this empowered European nations to acquire lands they "discovered" inhabited by non-Christian peoples. The indigenous residents lost the right to their land after the Europeans claimed it. Though originally applied by predominantly Roman Catholic nations, in 1792 Secretary of State Thomas Jefferson declared the Doctrine to be applicable in U.S. law as well. This policy has been referenced many times in U.S. courts, even as recently as the early 2000s, and has been used repeatedly to rob native peoples of what little land they still inhabit. Slowly the impact of the Doctrine has given way to rulings establishing indigenous people's sovereignty over the land, but it has been an ongoing fight.[19]

While all of these laws and acts have been challenged and later deemed unconstitutional, the fact that they were enacted at all betrays the underlying white-supremacist intent at the heart of the nation's founding documents. Moreover, while their legal status has been established, many if not all of the affected racial and ethnic groups still find that the underlying attitudes continue and affect them on a daily basis. This leads to the third major marker in the U.S. history of racism.

Parallel Competing Narratives

Kendi[20] states that the "inequality of the white and Black races [and one could add other non-European racial/ethnic groups] was stamped from the beginning."[21] The laws and policies discussed in the preceding section assured that subordinate status. Kendi goes on to show that throughout U.S. history there have been two parallel and competing themes of progress. The first, frequently mentioned by well-meaning whites (and even in Michelle Obama's speech discussed at the beginning of this chapter), is the idea that despite our white-supremacist past, we as a nation have made great strides toward racial equity. This is certainly true. Previous exclusionary and discriminatory laws and practices have been rescinded or changed.

While there has been racial progress, Kendi notes there has also been ongoing development of racist policies and practices. Almost every change toward greater freedom and access for BIPOC has been countered by laws and policies to limit it. Often when people have acted or spoken in a racist manner, the response has been that the person is just ignorant and in need of more education. Kendi contends that racism is not due to ignorance, but rather to racist laws and policies. "Racist policies have driven the history of racist ideas in America."[22] Usually those policies are the result of a desire for some sort of economic, political or social advantage.

Just a cursory look at the U.S. history of race-related laws reveals how true this is. Following the Civil War, Black men gained full citizenship and the right to vote through the 14th and 15th amendments to the Constitution. What followed was about a 10-year period of Reconstruction, where Blacks began to exercise those new rights. But in 1876, when Reconstruction was disassembled, the Jim Crow laws and Black Codes were enacted throughout the South, severely limiting the freedoms of Blacks to vote and do other normal citizenship acts. In response to the Great Migration of many Blacks fleeing the Jim Crow South, many northern cities' neighborhood restrictive covenants, redlining and other forms of racial cartels assured that racial minorities were limited to certain areas of the city and inhibited their ability to accumulate wealth.[23] The Civil Rights Movement of the 1950s and 1960s made great strides, but was followed by the development of the Republicans' "Southern Strategy," which purposely appeals to white Southerners' racial fears and prejudices. The Black Power movements of the 1970s led to Richard Nixon's War on Drugs that targeted inner-city African Americans in disproportionate numbers. This in turn led to the mass incarceration of Black and Brown people today.[24] The election of Barack Obama—the first African American president—in 2008 led to the formation of the Tea Party that became the foundation for Donald Trump's election, the most overtly racist president in modern times.

What Kendi clearly shows is that while the U.S. has certainly made progress in some areas of race relations, such advances were often followed by efforts to turn back those gains. As discussed in Chapter 4, Richard Hughes asserts that "the Myth of White Supremacy is the primal American myth that informs all the others."[25] Like Kendi, Hughes believes that racism is something that we as a nation must continually contend with because it has pervaded our history and shaped who we are and how we see ourselves as white persons and BIPOC. This leads us then to consider our personal stories and how racism has shaped us as individuals.

The History that Shapes Our Experience

The reason for knowing and appreciating the history of racism is because in so many ways that history has shaped our personal experiences whether we are aware of it or not. That impact is not only seen in what people see and directly experience, but also what is absent from their awareness of it. For most white people, the most profound impact of the history of white supremacy is how it has prevented them from seeing how racism shaped their lives.

For instance, why have a majority of whites in this country grown up in predominantly white communities? In particular, why have the people living in suburbs surrounding most major cities been predominantly white? Why do most public-school students for the most part attend racially homogenous—white or students of color—school districts more than 60 years after the Supreme Court decision to desegregate? And why do school districts that have predominantly students of color receive significantly less funding than generally white school districts?[26]

Most white people have grown up amidst these historic discrepancies and yet are largely unaware of them. When such inequities are brought to light, all too often white leaders justify the disparities by implying and suggesting that BIPOC are lazy, socially inept, racially inferior and culturally deprived. While certain laws like redlining have been abolished, their effect—segregated neighborhoods—remains. In many states, economic, educational and political inequities are "locked in" by laws and policies that make it difficult to change them. White people are given advantages by the laws, structures and policies of institutions they did not know about or ask for.[27]

In other cases, the decisions by political and business leaders have been more deliberate and focused. Michelle Alexander[28] reveals how Presidents Nixon and Reagan specifically targeted communities of color in the "War on Crime" and "War on Drugs." These approaches led to a disproportionate percentage of young men of color being incarcerated and subsequently deprived of basic citizenship rights like voting and access to housing. In more recent years, Republican leaders have engaged in active attempts at voter suppression, thus inhibiting BIPOC from their right to vote. For instance, in May 2017 the Supreme Court struck down a North Carolina voting law that they said was unconstitutional and a clear attempt to "target African Americans with almost surgical precision."[29] In Alabama, state officials restricted the forms of identification that could be used, and closed several polling stations in predominantly Black communities.[30] Even in these more pernicious cases, a majority of white people have been oblivious to such racially motivated actions and the resulting impact on their experience and understanding of racism.

As I think of my own story with regard to racism in this context, I am struck how—as a young person growing up in suburban Minneapolis—I was largely oblivious to the impact of these issues on my life. I grew up in an all-white community with an excellent public school. The BIPOC lived way on the other side of the city, a place from which I was warned to stay away. Because I was in sports, at times our school would visit the other schools, which seemed rundown compared to my school, but I never wondered, nor was I encouraged to, why there were such disparities. In 1971, I attended a university in a southern state and only learned years later that the few students of color in my class were only the eighth class in which African American undergraduates were admitted. When I was there, I simply knew there were very few Black students in my school.

Like many white people in my generation and in previous and subsequent ones, my life was prescribed by white supremacy ingrained in the institutions I attended, the opportunities I was offered and the resources available to me. White supremacy shaped how I thought of myself in relationship to others, who my friends and neighbors would be and the experiences I had growing up. Only by probing their own stories and the forces that shaped them can white persons come to terms with the impact that racism has had on their lives. And if they want to help other white people understand that impact, they must first understand its influence on themselves.

History Interacting with Our Stories

If we are to engage whites to consider the impact of the racist dynamics of history on their lives, we must begin by probing and understanding our own stories with regard to race. In recent years, there has been a renewed interest in tracking one's family history. Databases like Ancestry .com have enabled millions of people to trace their family lines through the centuries back to their origins in other countries. However, what is omitted in these searches is an awareness of the racial and ethnic context in which one's ancestors lived. A fuller picture would include information about what happened when one's European ancestors interacted with Native Americans, African slaves and other ethnic groups in U.S. history.

Edward Ball is the descendant of a prominent family from Charleston, South Carolina. He relates how his father often regaled him with stories of his famous ancestors, many of whom were large plantation owners who owned hundreds of slaves. When he was an adult and living out of the South, he was invited to a Ball family reunion, which included a boat trip up the Cooper River where the Ball plantations once stood. After the reunion, Ball decided to search out the stories of all the slaves whose names were forgotten and left unacknowledged in the family legacy. His book, *Slaves in My Family,* is his story of finding distant cousins descended from Ball plantation-owner slave rapes and the descendants of former slaves whose stories had been preserved.[31]

Ball's story, while unique to his family, is reflective of the history of near-ly all white Americans, which all too often involved enslaving, killing or removing other racial and ethnic groups, in turn contributing to inter-generational family wealth. White ancestors moving westward benefited from the Homestead Act of 1862, which provided thousands of families free land in the western territories, but denied that same opportunity to African Americans.[32] The arrival of white settlers on land inhabited by Native Americans often led to their removal from those lands. White communities and schools were "protected" by laws and housing cove-nants that excluded families of color from moving in. At the same time, some whites have in their family history individuals who fought and suf-fered for racial justice as part of the Underground Railroad network, participated in the abolitionist movement or joined the marches for civil rights in the mid-20th century.[33]

Our personal race histories interact with the larger history of racism in the United States, which certainly includes stories of bravery, ingenui-ty and hard work. Yet at the same time that history also includes a for-gotten legacy of degradation, dehumanization and death of others. As the author William Faulkner said: "The past is never dead. It's not even past."[34] Whether or not we know that part of our story, it still has shaped and affects us.[35]

Section 2
Engaging White People

Start with Their Story and Listen:
The Transformative Power of Dialogue

To be human is to tell stories.

—M. Carolyn Clark

The Meeting

On May 12, 1963, author and essayist James Baldwin sent an urgent telegram to Robert F. Kennedy—attorney general of the United States—about the "chaos in Birmingham." For several months, the African American citizens of Birmingham, Alabama, had been boycotting retail stores in that city because of the dehumanizing treatment they had been receiving from local store owners. The boycott, which started in 1962, had begun to have an effect, causing white retailers to lose 40% of their normal revenue. In early 1963, the Southern Christian Leadership Conference (SCLC) under Dr. Martin Luther King, Jr., joined the boycott and urged the Black citizens of Birmingham to boycott white-owned stores for the six weeks leading up to Easter, the second-largest shopping season of the year. Storeowners began to take down their "Whites Only" signs and change their discriminatory practices, but Commissioner of Public Safety Bull Connor threatened to revoke the storeowners' licenses if they gave in to the SCLC and boycotters' demands.

What followed was a series of sit-ins, marches and protests in which hundreds of people including youth, small children and Dr. King himself were arrested and put in jail. The protestors' goal was to fill the jails and thereby cripple the city apparatus. Bull Connor brought out dogs and hoses and brutally beat the protestors. Then on the eve of Mother's Day, May 11th, bombs were set off at the home of A.D. King, Dr. King's brother and the hotel where Dr. King and his advisors were staying. In retaliation, Blacks threw rocks at store windows, burned down shops and attacked police officers. The situation was devolving quickly.[1]

Baldwin's telegram warned that the racial violence in Birmingham was "neither regional; nor racial. It's a matter of the nation's life or death; no truce can be binding until the American people and our representatives are able to accept the simple fact that the Negro is a man."[2] Kennedy responded by inviting Baldwin to meet with him the next day at his home in Washington, DC. Over breakfast, Kennedy asked Baldwin to arrange a meeting with "the Negroes that other Negroes listen to," but insisted that Black politicians like Adam Clayton Powell or activists like Dr. King not be invited.[3] Baldwin agreed and gathered a group to meet with Kennedy that included Baldwin's lawyer Clarence Jones, singer Harry Belafonte, playwright Lorraine Hansberry, psychologist Kenneth Clark, singer Lena Horne and Freedom Rider Jerome Smith.

On May 24, 1963, the group gathered in an apartment the Kennedy family owned in New York City. After some light banter and pleasantries, Kennedy began listing all the important actions his brother's administration had taken on behalf of "Negroes and civil rights."[4] He also pointed out that the strong resistance to these efforts by Southern Democrats "had the [Democratic] party in revolt."[5] He argued that Black leaders needed to go slow, be grateful for the progress that had been made and seek steady improvement. He expressed concern that Blacks were being influenced by extremist elements like the Black Muslims, whom he felt were "stirring up trouble." When Kennedy said this, Jerome Smith—having experienced severe beatings on his Freedom Ride—responded, "You have no idea what trouble is," relating the violence he had endured in simply riding a bus.[6] This led the others to join in and what followed was an extensive expression of pent-up frustration and rage.

According to Michael Eric Dyson, "Kennedy had never witnessed Black pain like this before in such naked, unglossed ferocity. The Black folk in the room largely let rage run free, for a moment at least, before one of the most powerful white men in the world."[7] Kennedy felt attacked and fumed in response to their anger. Kenneth Clark noted that "Bobby sat immobile in the chair: he no longer continued to defend himself. He just sat and you could see the tension and the pressure building in him."[8] They denounced the FBI, Kennedy's Department of Justice and the overall halfhearted efforts of the Kennedy administration to address the injustices being experienced by Blacks in the Civil Rights Movement. Every time Kennedy tried to defend his administration's policies and actions, they were denounced as insufficient. Feeling demoralized and disgusted, Kennedy ended the meeting. He left discouraged that Blacks were not interested in policy, but only in sharing their stories and calling attention to various atrocities.

However, after Kennedy calmed down and reflected on the pain and rage he had heard in the meeting, he started to consider the truth of what they were telling him. Dyson writes, "In short order, the encounter with this group of extraordinary black folk would begin to haunt him; it would help change his mind and therefore history.... Bobby turned his resentment into resolve and got even more determined to make substantive change.... "[9] Dyson continues:

> But on this day, in this meeting, something different happened: the unvarnished, unfiltered truth got loose; the reality of black perception without blinders or shades became clear; the beautiful ugliness of our existence got vented without being dressed up and made presentable, or amenable, or acceptable to white ears. That's why the meeting made headlines, made front page, made history and finally made the white man listen.[10]

Dyson concludes:

> In fact, the brutal battering [Kennedy] suffered at the hands of the Baldwin crew offers an important lesson to white people about how to start real change. And that involves sometimes sitting silently and finally, as black folk have been forced to do, listening and listening and listening and listening some more.[11]

Getting White People to Listen

While there is no doubt in my mind that the rage expressed that day was justified and, while I unequivocally agree that whites need to hear the pain experienced by Blacks and other peoples of color, I also know that most white people are not like Robert Kennedy, who was able to step back from his initial defensiveness and critically reflect on what he was being told. That is why Bobby Kennedy became the most outspoken white politician of his generation for racial justice and civil rights before his tragic death in 1968.

Unfortunately, most white people in Kennedy's position would have remained angry and defensive, and distanced themselves as much as possible from Baldwin and his colleagues. Unlike Kennedy, most white people in America have been taught to fear, resist, deny and avoid at all costs the truth of racism. So while I agree with Dyson that whites need to hear and confront the truth of racism, it will most likely not come through dramatic confrontations, but rather by means that invite whites to explore and reflect on the ways in which they have been shaped by their upbringing, their education and their skewed perceptions of race and racism.

I recognize there are times when the only option one has is to call out white peers for their racist words or actions.[12] Sometimes people in positions of power, like Bobby Kennedy, must be confronted with the truth. At the same time, even those times of confrontation need to be complemented with a more dialogical approach that encourages and invites white people to consider their words, actions, thoughts and feelings, and the experiences and influences that have shaped their attitudes toward BIPOC, race and racism. This chapter offers a model of how storytelling and dialogue can be used to engage white people in meaningful and transformative conversations about racism.

The NewCORE Method[13]

For the past several years I have been part of an interracial, interfaith group called NewCORE (New Conversations on Race and Ethnicity).[14] Once a month for a couple of hours, a racially and religiously diverse group of people meet to discuss issues of the day and share personal experiences dealing with racism. Over the years, the group has developed an approach to conversation built around personal storytelling, active empathic listening, asking probing questions and dialogue.

NewCORE's origin stems from a 2008 speech delivered in Philadelphia by then-Senator Barack Obama titled "A More Perfect Union." In it, he discussed race in America and issued a challenge to the nation to engage in sincere conversation on race. Later that same year, Dr. Cornel West was invited to Philadelphia and urged his listeners to take up the challenge Obama offered. In the audience that night was Philadelphia Mayor Michael Nutter, who shortly after West's visit gathered a group of religious leaders, including leading African American clergy, Jewish rabbis and the director of the city's Office of Faith-Based Initiatives. Nutter told the group that he wanted Philadelphia, a city historically torn by racial strife, to have this conversation and asked the faith leaders to consider how that might be brought into being.

For several months, a small group of clergy met to discuss how they could help the city have a meaningful conversation about race. At first, they thought about developing an approach, a template of sorts, that could be adapted by various groups. One of the questions they grappled with was who did they want to reach; should they seek to train police officers, firefighters, people involved in situations where racial incidents had occurred, people seeking antiracism training and/or others? They were not sure. By this time, the group had grown to a healthy mix of about 25 people grappling with these issues. In the room each month were represented some of the major religious organizations in the city, most of which were contending with racism within their own institutions. Eventually the group came to the uncomfortable realization that they were not in a position to tell others how to undo racism; they were leaders of institutions plagued with unresolved racial issues. They realized that they had to do their own work on the racism within themselves and their organizations before they could instruct anyone else how to carry on a constructive conversation about race.

One person who had been part of the ongoing meetings offered a simple suggestion: "Let's get to know one another first and share our experiences and struggles with racism. Let's create a space where people can share their stories and be supported and guided as they grapple with their pain and questions related to race." And so began a monthly practice of one group member sharing his or her story while others listened and then asked questions designed to probe those experiences more deeply, within a context of support and communal reflection. Over the next several years following this approach, what came to be called the NewCORE Method™ emerged.

Essentially it begins with these questions: "Who are you? How do you understand yourself in terms of race and gender? What are the experiences and influences that led you to that understanding?" While a designated person is telling his or her personal story, the others in the room are encouraged to engage in active, intentional listening in a way that communicates openness and empathy to the storyteller. When the person has finished sharing, the group is invited to ask questions in a very particular way; they are encouraged to resist the temptation to tell their own story and instead probe the storyteller's account, inviting him or her to go deeper.

Listeners are encouraged to ask honest, open-ended questions that don't anticipate a particular answer, but rather invite the storyteller to expand on and deepen his or her story. This avoids trying to give advice, relate similar personal experiences or make a statement in the form of a question. Effective questions are brief and seek to serve the storyteller and not one's personal curiosity. They focus not just on facts but feelings, interpretations and perspectives, and allow the storyteller to perhaps see things not realized before.[15]

As members of the group ask their open-ended questions, a broader dialogue develops, which is not about who is right or wrong, but rather draws everyone to a deeper understanding of the issues being discussed. The personal story invites exploration leading to dialogue, resulting in everyone coming to a fuller awareness of themselves and the impact that racism has had on them.

As this approach to conversation about race developed within the group meeting monthly, NewCORE members have been invited to lead groups in conversations around the city with this same approach. They have met in coffee shops, classrooms, government buildings, community centers and formal dinners, with people of all ages and racial/ethnic groups. In most cases, those who attended these events are open to having honest conversations about race. And through all of these experiences, they come to realize that many times their preconceived idea of the "other" is misguided.

The NewCORE Method™ is still evolving and not without flaws. However, its essence is to invite personal storytelling that can then open up dialogue about racism and how it has impacted them.

Tell Me a Story

I have sought to adapt the NewCORE Method for conversations with white people about race. I offer a framework that includes inviting people to share their stories, ask open-ended questions and engage in empathic listening that leads to dialogue. Usually when leading a group around a discussion about race and racism, I begin by asking people to think about the first time they became aware of race and how they came to understand racial identity. I then ask them to share a time when they either experienced or witnessed racism in some form. What follows are a series of stories, sometimes troubling and often painful, that tell a great deal about the person and impact race has had. For white people, very often simply telling the story can be difficult, because race has been such a taboo topic. Even that can be revealing, not only for those hearing the story, but for the person sharing as well.

For many white people, jumping into a conversation about race is too big a leap. That's why I begin with an invitation to tell one's story. Stories are the way in which human beings make sense out of the disordered confusion of their lives and derive meaning from their experiences. In effect, identity is shaped and determined by the stories one constructs and tells oneself. "Narrative understanding is our most primitive form of explanation. We make sense of things by fitting them into stories."[16]

Through the centuries, human beings have used stories to define personhood, moral values, the meaning of suffering and much more. When asked to explain how they are feeling, or why they think or act in a certain way, people often respond by telling a story. They select events and experiences, and form them into a sequence that conveys a deeper meaning as to why they think or feel as they do and the process that got them there. Depending on the context in which one is telling the story and the audience to whom it is being relayed, certain facts may be added or omitted, highlighted or downplayed.

However, stories are not only for the listener. More importantly, they are a tool for the tellers to help understand themselves better. Personal stories are a way of making sense of one's experiences. In fact, our personal identities, the ways in which we understand ourselves, are really the result of the stories we have created around those identities. Thus for every aspect of one's identity, be it son or daughter, parent or worker in a particular role, friend in a certain circle or member of a certain group, there is a story that explains how one came to inhabit that role and what it means.

This highlights another important aspect of storytelling: People learn from telling them. When verbalizing their story, they often hear and experience things that have not occurred to them. They discover that they are stronger or more confused about what they believe to be true than they thought. Sometimes telling one's story can evoke strong emotions in the storyteller. Tears, anger, laughter, excitement and other emotions often spontaneously emerge in a way that catches them by surprise. And as people experience their own story, they may decide to re-examine themselves and change. Storytelling is a powerful tool in conversations with white people about race because often in the telling and dialogue that follow, new insights emerge. What one thought to be true comes under question and what seemed certain before becomes more open to exploration.

Empathic Listening

When people tell their story, others must do what Steven Covey calls empathic listening. which requires them to "seek first to understand, then to be understood."[17] He points out that "most people don't listen with the intent to understand; they listen with the intent to reply."[18] By contrast, empathic listening seeks to understand other people's perspective, to actually attempt to get inside their skin to understand how they see and experience the world. The goal of empathy is not to agree with others, but to understand them both intellectually and emotionally. For the listener, empathy can be quite risky because it makes one vulnerable and possibly able to be influenced. However, the benefit is that by fully listening with empathy, one enables the other person to feel heard and opens up different perspectives. Empathetic listening gives us credibility with others and makes them more likely to hear our point of view.[19]

Too often conversations about race, especially with white people, involve a great deal of debating without much real listening. It's too easy to make assumptions about other people based on attitudes or political positions and they simply become adversaries to debate, rather than to understand. As a result, when someone makes a statement about race that I find offensive or off-putting, I respond with a question: "How did you come to that position? Tell me the story behind that statement. What happened that led you to that way of thinking?" And then I listen. Because I understand how whites are socialized to see people of other races, as well as white fragility and what leads to it, I understand there is a process that leads people to see the world that way. As difficult as it may be, I try to listen empathetically. And when the person finishes, I ask if I can tell how I came to see things the way I do; what could have ended up as a frustrating debate begins a dialogue—or series of dialogues—that can eventually lead to a deeper understanding of one another and personal change.

Invitation to Dialogue

Brazilian educator Paulo Freire provides us a framework for understanding effective dialogue.[20] While his insights on dialogue are generally presented in terms of the teacher-student relationship, his guidelines are equally applicable in conversations about race. He advocated dialogue as a teaching approach and an epistemological philosophy, in contrast to what he called the "banking approach" to teaching and learning, in which a person (like a teacher) sees himself or herself as the "expert" who then alternately "deposits" and imposes a certain way of understanding a topic and perceiving the world. The student is seen as an empty vessel, whose role is to passively receive what the expert provides without objection or question.

Unfortunately, all too many times discussions about race are approached by those who see themselves as more aware and enlightened on the topic, as "experts" whose job it is to educate and convince others the error of their ways and thinking. The expectation is that if others would come to understand issues the way the "expert" does, all would be well. However, more times than not, a heavy-handed, top-down, I-know-better-than-you approach provokes resistance and leads to anger, defensiveness, guilt and/or withdrawal.

Dialogue, by contrast and if handled well, invites the parties into a process of mutual exploration and understanding and assumes that they are equals on the same plane. Authentic dialogue also assumes that neither party will attempt to manipulate the other. Rather than trying to dominate with superior ideas through some sort of debating approach, dialogue begins with each individual's understanding of experiences and perceptions of the world. Dialogue involves listening so as to understand the other's perspective and to explore together its deeper and more complex dimensions, as well as asking questions with the aim of engaging in examining their views more critically. Freire even says that if one person in a dialogue has in fact more experience or understanding than the other, he or she relearns the topic afresh and the dialogue "seals [the two people] in the act of knowing and reknowing."[21]

Freire believed that through authentic, respectful dialogue, one not only comes to know the other person, but also to know oneself better. A person understands his or her "self" in dialogue with the "other." In dialogue, people can see things about others that they cannot see in themselves. At the same time, the other person can see things about that person they cannot see themselves. I come to know my whole self only as others share their perception of me and they only come to understand themselves fully by my dialogue with them.

Dr. Greg Ellison[22] calls such interactions "fearless dialogues" that may include fear in talking about difficult topics, which is diminished in an atmosphere of openness, mutual curiosity and hospitality. The key in Ellison's words is that dialogue partners truly see one another, that they are open to sharing their stories and being open to hear the experiences of those who might be quite different from them.

By proposing a dialogical approach to talking with white people about race issues, I am in no way suggesting that this is a soft or easy way for whites to deal with the effects of white supremacy on their lives. In fact, I am suggesting what Boler and Zembylas[23] call a "pedagogy of discomfort."[24] Talking about racism can be uncomfortable. When deeply held values and cherished myths, such as American exceptionalism and meritocracy, are challenged, people have a tendency to resist what is being said. Dialogue doesn't remove the discomfort but invites one to move through it.

Key Dimensions of Effective Dialogue

In authentic dialogue, one doesn't seek to force views on other people or tell them what to think, but approaches each encounter with openness to other views and the possibility of learning oneself. Freire identifies four key factors that contribute to authentic dialogue. First, dialogue is *profoundly loving* toward the world and other people. One engages in dialogues about race first because they care deeply for those who are continually dehumanized by individual acts and systematic racism in our society. At the same time, they must sincerely care for the other person with whom they are talking. As Ellison says: "One must train the ear, intensify the imagination and expand the levels of empathy to hear value in the stories of others who are as much in need of liberation as the oppressed."[25] Only love will entice others to consider new ways of thinking and seeing the world.

Second, dialogue requires *humility*. Too often in confrontations on race people can fall into a kind of elitism, that "I know better than the other." Freire would caution us to remain humble, aware that we are still in a process of learning and transformation, even as we seek to invite others to that process. He writes: "Self-sufficiency is incompatible with dialogue."[26] With humility comes curiosity and an openness to the other person. Authentic humility is interested in the other. Moreover, humility opens one up to learning things oneself and at least to gain a critical awareness of how others perceive the world.

Third, authentic dialogue requires *faith in people to change and to change the world around them*, that no one is stuck in a particular place and position. Dialogue requires *trust* and over time can build trust, even when discussing difficult topics. Closely related to faith and trust is *hope*. Freire calls hope an "ontological need" and "a concrete imperative" that people need to make it through the hard struggles of life. People must believe there is a better way.[27] As hard as it may seem at times when having these difficult conversations, one must remain hopeful that progress is being made, even if the other person seems resistant.

Finally, authentic dialogue leads the parties involved to *engage in critical thinking* about their experiences, views on issues, and assumptions about people and the world. The way to encourage this is what he calls "problem-posing," an approach in which probing questions are asked that prompt people to think more deeply about what they say they think and believe. There are a number of conscious and unconscious inherited myths and stereotypes about people of other races that need to be brought to the surface and examined. There are also assumptions about how systems and institutions work that need to be interrogated. Dialogue is not just about becoming more comfortable with and learning about one another; it's about examining one's values, beliefs and received knowledge.

While Freire stresses love, respect and openness to others in the process of dialogue, its ultimate goal is personal and societal change: "Dialogue is an encounter among people mediated by the world, in order to name the world"[28] For Freire, to name the world is to exert power over one's circumstances, thus to name the world means that one has the ability to change it. Through dialogue, people are invited to critical self-reflection on their attitudes, values and worldview. By moving from what he calls naïve consciousness (a very surface-level way of thinking) to a more critical view, Freire contends that people begin to understand issues in a different way and are moved to act against injustice and the attitudes and perspectives that contribute to that injustice. In this sense, dialogue is a calculated gamble that conversation will lead to greater awareness, to change and ultimately to action.

This gamble involves facing what Freire calls "limit situations"—internal and external barriers that impede people from changing their thinking and acting in different ways. Those perceived barriers may be fears of interacting with people who appear to be different. They may involve concerns about what family or friends might say if people changed their views. A person may fear losing friends, being criticized or in some way excluded. These are real barriers in the sense that they can hold people back, but are not impassable. Freire says when people experience these limit situations they face "real boundaries where all possibilities begin."[29] It's like when a child walks for the first time, standing and haltingly taking the first step, then another and another, until going all the way across the room. Dialogue invites us to take the risk of stepping past that perceived boundary to the new possibilities that exist. For many white people, race is one such perceived boundary. And dialogue invites them to step into the water to see what might be possible in their relationships with people of other races and ethnicities.

Also, when one is listening to another person who says something the listener feels is "wrong," there is a natural tendency to shut down and stop listening. One has to exercise great emotional intelligence by recognizing that certain comments can be emotional triggers. The challenge is to channel one's emotions from anger or discomfort to a question that pushes the storyteller to go deeper. That's not always easy or possible to do. Freire speaks of the need for tolerance in dialogue, which he describes as "the virtue that teaches us to live with the different. It teaches us to learn from and respect the different."[30]

Even so, openness to another's way of thinking or acting is not without limits. Freire says: "Being tolerant does not mean acquiescing to the intolerable; it does not mean covering up disrespect; it does not mean coddling the aggressor or disguising the aggression."[31] Despite our desire to be inviting and encouraging, there are times when we need to call each other out for things said or done. Hopefully, by approaching the conversation of race dialogically, one can earn the trust to say a hard word.

Having Conversations on Race

I am suggesting that we utilize an approach like the NewCORE Method that uses storytelling, empathetic listening and dialogue as a way to talk about issues of race. In the following chapters, I highlight some common responses to racism expressed by white people and how we can engage those issues and people with a dialogical approach.

Over the past three decades, I have had countless conversations about race with students, colleagues, family members, friends and critics of what I may say, write or do. We especially need to have these conversations with white people. Far too many times when the topic of racism is raised, people engage in labeling, finger pointing and debating "facts" that leave everyone angry, frustrated, unconvinced and unchanged. Over time I have come to the conviction that the NewCORE approach—the process of storytelling, listening and dialogue—is the way to engage the conversation with other white people.

As stated in the introductory chapter, I agree with those BIPOC who insist that white people need to do their own work on racism. If the U.S. white community is ever going to move past its pervasive fear, guilt, defensiveness and anger about racial issues, there are going to have to be significant numbers of people willing to engage their white friends, coworkers, family members and casual acquaintances in conversations about race.

The following chapters explore how this approach can be used to engage white people in meaningful conversations about racism in spite of the many excuses, diversions and barriers they present. So let us turn to that now.

Responding to Claims of Colorblindness

When you say you don't see race, you are saying you don't see me.
—African American graduate student

A Casual Conversation

One day I was talking with a white woman who works as a clerk in a store that I frequent. In a casual conversation, I told her that I was writing a book about how to talk to white people about race. She responded by telling me about her white son and his two Black friends. She said she felt good that he had developed friendships with boys of another race. One night her son was talking about his friends and referred to them as "Black." When she heard her son say that, she was horrified and told him that he should not refer to people by their race.

I asked her why she was horrified. She explained that she had been raised to believe that to refer to people by their race was racist. I then asked her why she felt her son's words were racist and it became clear that this was something she had been raised to believe.

Colorblindness

What this woman had innocently demonstrated is what is referred to as colorblindness, "the belief, stated or implied through actions, that the ultimate goal in ending racial discrimination is best served 'by treating individuals qua individuals—that is, on the 'content of their character not the color of their skin'."[1] And for many if not most whites, to be color-blind is to "not see race" and thereby avoid appearing racist.

Colorblindness manifests itself in statements such as "I don't see race; I just see people," "I am colorblind," "The only race is the human race" and "To speak of a person's race is to be racist." In each of these re-sponses, there is an implied commitment to not see race or even a denial that race actually exists. However, as discussed earlier in this book, racism is a fact of life in U.S. society today. As in Chapter 2, race is a social construct, not a biological one, but that doesn't erase the history of slavery, Jim Crow and ongoing racial oppression. To deny that race exists is to ignore the very real impact that race and racism have had on people's lived experiences. As Frederick Herzog says: "Being colorblind ... easily can mean becoming blind to the savage struggle those of another color are caught in."[2]

Changing Language Without Dealing with Racism

Most whites I encounter who exhibit this tendency toward colorblindness don't do so out of any apparent malice or disrespect. In fact, in most cases they are intentionally trying to avoid doing or saying anything overtly racist. In their minds they are seeking to live out Dr. King's call to judge people not by the color of their skin, but by the content of their character; the Civil Rights Movement is largely attributed to ushering in this tendency among many whites toward colorblindness.

During the Civil Rights Movement and before, it was quite common for whites to speaking openly and disparagingly of Black and Brown people. Derogatory epithets and labels were common in public society. But with the passage of civil-rights legislation and whites' increasing awareness of racial equality, those derogatory characterizations of nonwhite people became less acceptable in general society. Today, in most companies people can be disciplined or even lose their job if they utter racial epithets in the workplace. While employers cannot police what an employee thinks, they can restrict what an employee says and does toward people of other races. Thus, most whites regardless of attitude have adopted what they consider to be raceless, race-neutral or colorblind phrasing when speaking of people of other races.[3]

The problem is that despite the linguistic change, racism still operates freely in a more covert manner. This "colorblind racism"[4] avoids the use of racial terminology and instead uses "code words" when speaking of BIPOC.

This tendency toward covert racism has become widespread in the political realm and results in what Ian Haney Lopez[5] calls "dog-whistle politics," whereby politicians use disparaging racially coded images such as "welfare queen," "super-predator," "drug dealers" and the like in reference to BIPOC without ever directly referring to race. In fact, over the last 50 years the Republican party has employed a Southern Strategy designed to appeal to racist attitudes without ever uttering a racially charged word.[6] In a similar manner, many if not most white people avoid using racially charged language, but that does mean racism is still not very much present in their attitudes and actions.[7]

Colorblind Racism

Dr. Eduardo Bonilla-Silva, professor of sociology ay Duke University, interviewed over 1000 people, both Black and white, on their attitudes toward various social and racial issues.[8] From this study, he identified what he called a "new racism" or what has been more commonly called "colorblind racism," which is distinguished from the more overt racism of the civil-rights era and earlier. By comparison, it appears to be "racism lite" operating in ways that are "subtle, institutional and apparently nonracial"[9] in that this new form of racism does nothing to address white privilege or the laws, policies and systems that support it. "Shielded by colorblindness, whites can express resentment toward minorities; criticize their morality and work ethic; and even claim to be victims of reverse racism."[10]

Colorblindness manifests itself in a variety of ways. In some cases, whites explain disparities between whites and BIPOC by asserting that all people are equal and attribute differences in social and economic standing to individual choices and efforts without mentioning the social and economic factors influencing the impact of one's individual actions. Others attribute differences to natural tendencies or even genetics, and to factors such as "a culture of poverty," poor family structures or inherent tendencies toward laziness or violence. This cultural racism substitutes culture for race in explaining disparities. Finally, some whites simply minimize the importance of race and past discrimination and attribute racial disparities to other factors such as class or education. The common factor in all of these rationalizations is that they never call into question the systemic and economic factors at play.[11]

Colorblind racism uses a variety of linguistic and logical strategies to deny or hide the impact of racism, while enabling whites to maintain their sense of innocence about benefiting from the racist policies and laws at work to create disparities. My observation in many predominantly white social settings is that conversations often stop or change directions when the issue of racism is raised. Another approach often used by whites is to come up with all sorts of factors other than race for what was clearly a racist act, or to simply attribute the racist actions of other whites to ignorance, asserting if otherwise "good" white people knew more they would not have done or said what they did. Finally, some whites will recognize that an action or person is racist, but then act as if nothing can be done to change people's attitudes and actions. All of these responses are usually unconscious, yet result in whites claiming racial innocence, protecting their identities and the privilege that goes with it.[12]

For these reasons, claims of colorblindness are demeaning and destructive to BIPOC. At the same time, it's also detrimental to white people. Colorblind racism prevents whites from honestly and critically examining their racial beliefs, values, emotions and actions. It alienates them from BIPOC, makes it difficult to empathize and causes them to disengage from honest conversations with BIPOC.[13] In many of my courses where racism is a topic to be examined, I have assigned students to have a conversation or series of conversations with a person of another race and/or ethnicity. On several occasions, students have chosen someone they considered to be a close friend as their dialogue partner. Even so, they reported that they had not talked about racial issues with that friend and learned things they had never known about the other—even though they had supposedly been friends for a long period of time. By ignoring the reality of their racial differences, these supposedly good friends missed out on knowing many racial factors impacting their lives.

Addressing Colorblind Racism
So in talking with white people, when one encounters claims of colorblindness, how can he or she use that occasion to help them become aware of what they are doing and its impact on the BIPOC around them? I usually start by asking for an explanation: "What do you mean when

you say you don't see race, that you are colorblind?" How we ask the question is critical. We are not accusing people of anything, but rather seeking to fully understand what *they* mean by colorblindness. As stated above, when whites claim not to see race or consider it a significant factor, they actually believe they are demonstrating that they are not racist.

Once their good intentions have been established, people should explore their concrete experiences with persons of another race. One might ask questions such as the following:

- Why do you feel it's important to not call attention to another person's race?
- Do you have any friends or coworkers of another race? What are those relationships like? Have you ever discussed racial issues with them? Have you acknowledged that you are of different races? What was that like?
- How did you develop the perspective that it's non-racist to be "colorblind?" How have you felt when people bring up the topic of race when you are with both BIPOC and other white people?
- Have you ever been in a situation where you were a racial minority? How did it feel to be one of the only white people in the room? How did it feel when you left that setting?

The point of these questions and others like them is to call attention to the fact that they do see race, with powerful attached feelings such as anxiety, fear, guilt and anger. As I will discuss in a later chapter, it's important to acknowledge these feelings and to stress that while uncomfortable, they are perfectly understandable given the history of racism in this country.

After one has had the opportunity to acknowledge the reality of race and the feelings it stirs up, it also becomes important to point out that despite the positive intentions, many BIPOC take offense at claims of colorblindness. One time in a course I was teaching, a white male made claims of colorblindness and I turned to the African Americans in the class and asked them to respond. One woman clearly explained that to deny race is to deny the history of racism in the country and the continuing racism that Black people deal with every day. She went on to explain that if he claimed not to see race, he was denying an important part of her identity. In so doing, he was saying he did not see her. While the man's intention was to avoid racism, in fact he had touched a nerve. While this was a particularly poignant moment, I have repeatedly heard similar statements made by BIPOC. In that situation, I had the luxury of having several BIPOC in the room who were able to speak to the issue. But often these statements are made in predominantly white settings and then it becomes our job to share the impact of colorblind claims on BIPOC.

We also cannot predict how people will respond to our questions. In his study, Bonilla-Silva noticed what he called "the linguistics of colorblind racism." In essence, each of these responses is intended maintain one's racial innocence, that they had just made a mistake. Some responses they might give would be as follows:

- I am not prejudiced, or some of my friends/family are prejudiced but not me.
- I am not Black/Latinx/Asian/Native American, so how would I know what it feels like?
- I see what you mean, but that's not what I meant (and so I should be exonerated).
- Sometimes people are just too uptight about race.
- Black, Brown, Native Americans and other people of color live too much in the past.

The purpose behind responses like these is to deny the existence of racism, rather than examining what racism is and how it has shaped their worldview. Because for some whites the topic of race is so uncomfortable, they can make irrational statements that are simply trying to avoid the topic altogether. When a white person is deeply entrenched in colorblind attitudes and language, it's important to recognize that the ultimate goal is to save face by not appearing racist. Because of the structure of racism, whites have been thoroughly socialized into colorblind thinking and acting, no matter how illogical and dysfunctional it may appear.

However, by raising open-ended questions as I have suggested, we give white people an opportunity to examine their attitudes and where they came from.[14]

If people asking the question are other whites, they should acknowledge that they also subscribed to colorblindness at one time in their life. It's important to share the story of how they changed and what influenced them. In such times, it's crucial to affirm one's own development in racial awareness as a sign and goal for others. On the other hand, if people asking the questions are BIPOC, it's equally important that they share their personal reactions to claims of colorblindness and how it impacts them. The stronger the case we make against colorblindness based on our personal experiences, the more likely it is that others will examine their own attitudes. Moreover, hopefully we have opened the door for further conversations that will help whites understand how deeply, though unwittingly, they may have been influenced by the forces of white supremacy in the way they think and act.

Conclusion

In this chapter, we have examined the phenomena of colorblindness and colorblind racism, and the ways they reinforce white privilege and white supremacy in the society at large. We have seen how whites make claims to colorblindness thinking they are avoiding being racist, but actually are suppressing their private thoughts and feelings around race. We have also explored how whites express themselves in confusing and paradoxical ways, such that they deceive themselves into thinking they are hiding their biases, when in fact they are not. Indeed, the whole purpose behind claims of colorblindness and "not seeing race" is to make a positive appearance, no matter what actually lies beneath the surface. We have then discussed various open-ended questions designed to get whites to think critically about their own attitudes and actions. We have also reviewed the kind of responses that might be given to avoid doing that self-examination.

In the end, one conversation won't convert a person claiming not to see race into an antiracist advocate. Calling attention to the absurdity of claiming not to see race may cause people to avoid the topic altogether. However, by approaching the person and topic with empathy and an awareness of the dynamics at play, the hope is that we might begin a conversation that can lead to further opportunities for discussion and growth.

Guilt, Shame and Denial

*No curtain under heaven is heavier than that curtain
of guilt and lies behind which Americans hide.*

—James Baldwin

Overwhelmed and Hopeless

In her book, *Why Are All the Black Kids Sitting Together in the Cafeteria*, Dr. Beverly Tatum[1] describes her experience teaching a course, "The Psychology of Racism," explaining that when the topic of racism was discussed, her white students often became bound up with a deep sense of guilt and hopelessness. Like Dr. Tatum, over the years I have found—both in classroom and workshop settings—that when white people begin to gain an awareness of the reality of racism and their part in it, they often slip into a profound sense of guilt. Even those who want to deny the reality of racism in American society, or in their lives, will defend themselves by accusing me of trying to make them feel guilty, when all I have done is mentioned the words "race" and "racism."

When white people begin to grasp the way in which racism is intertwined in their personal and professional lives, and attitudes, perceptions, institutional policies and laws that govern their lives, their worldview starts to crumble. When they confront the historical myths that have been propagated by educational institutions, political leaders and even faith communities, that realization can be devastating. With the sense of guilt come feelings of confusion, powerlessness and hopelessness.

I once led a workshop for some recently graduated college students. In the group was a young man who had obviously done some reading and given a great deal of thought toward how to become antiracist in his thinking and actions. He said: "I feel so overwhelmed and often guilty. How can I work on being antiracist without feeling so awful?"

In other settings with friends and colleagues, the response has sometimes been more hostile. In one conversation, I painstakingly sought to outline the systemic and institutional nature of racism. I concluded by saying that because of social and cultural influences, by design all whites carry racist attitudes and beliefs. I included myself in that statement, calling myself a recovering racist. My friend responded angrily, "So you are saying I'm racist!" (Yes, I was.) In his mind, I had accused him of something horrible and unthinkable. However, I did so not as an accusation but rather as a diagnosis and description of our collective condition as white people.

The Reality of Guilt

Given the history of the United States with regard to slavery, Jim Crow laws, policies seeking to exclude people of various racial and ethnic groups, and even current U.S. policies and actions regarding Muslims, immigrants and refugees, the collective guilt of American whites is an historical and political fact.[2] As has been discussed, the effects of that history are seen in disparities of intergenerational wealth, the geographical locations where people of different races live, disproportionate rates of disease, evidence of race-based mass incarceration and much more. Because of that history, there are still laws in effect that disproportionately impact BIPOC negatively as compared to whites. Whether individual whites directly benefited from past atrocities, white people as a group have received significant advantages due to the policies and practices designed to give advantage to their whiteness.

The pain of recognizing one's participation in—and benefiting from—racism is so intense because it causes whites to question and challenge so many aspects of their lives they thought were just "normal." The most hideous dimension of historic and systemic racism is that white privilege and power led them to believe that their worldview and way of life is the norm by which all other racial groups must be evaluated. To realize that lie can be devastating.

Guilt is also a deep and painful emotion, involving accepting responsibility for violating a moral standard. It's deeply uncomfortable and generally moves one to make efforts to rectify the guilt-inducing situation. White guilt can be defined as a *general sense of unease felt by white people who see their racial group as responsible for the advantages they possess over and against other racial groups.*[3] As an emotion, white guilt is generally experienced when a person is either confronted with information of past and current expressions of racism, or has a compelling interaction with a BIPOC wherein one becomes aware of feelings or beliefs that reveal personal prejudice. As discussed in Chapter 2, this second incidence is described as aversive racism, when one recognizes previously unaware beliefs and attitudes.[4]

Forms and Responses of Guilt

While some commentators, like conservative author Shelby Steele,[5] have suggested that the current emphasis on racial justice has afflicted white Americans with an ongoing sense of guilt, most scholars who have studied this phenomenon contend that short of some sort of precipitating incident, most whites don't carry around such guilt about the U.S. history of racism or its prevalence of racist acts in the present.[6] Whites tend to be very individualistic and present-oriented in their worldview, so they don't take responsibility for past events like slavery or Jim Crow laws, nor do they see a connection between their status in society and incidents in the news, government policies or legal decisions. Their socialization and education has led them to have a general trust in current laws and policies that blinds them to the injustices. So when guilt does arise because of a jolting awareness, it comes as an unexpected and unwelcome intruder.

Personal Guilt

In her studies of racial-identity development, Dr. Janet Helms[7] found that when white people become aware of racial prejudice and discrimination in themselves, the people around them and/or the organizations of which they are a part, they enter into what she called the stage of disintegration, when whites become aware of their whiteness and the inherent privilege and racial advantage that comes with it. This "triggers the moral dilemmas associated with being white."[8] Whites begin to question what they were taught to believe about race, racism and BIPOC. They may see for the first time that whites and BIPOC are not regarded and treated equally as they had been led to believe. As Helms says, "Once the silence is broken, the cycle of racism becomes increasingly visible."[9]

With this new awareness comes emotional discomfort characterized by feelings of guilt, sadness and powerlessness to change anything. Whites becomes aware of prejudices and assumptions they have carried all their life, often unconsciously. They are more sensitive to racist comments and actions by people close to them, such as friends, co-workers and members of their families. For instance, when I was growing up, my father would often tell a story about my mother driving her convertible with the top down through Harlem with her blond son (me) in the back seat. As a child, I thought this was a story of how silly my mom had been. However, when I became more aware of racism, that story took on a painful meaning about my father's racial fear of Black people and the communities where they live. Even if significant persons in one's life had not done or said anything overtly racist, the very denial of race as a key construct in American society leaves one blind to racism. Having one's eyes open to this denial of racism can be a painful shock.

Helms says that this new awareness creates dissonance between what people believe to be true and the new reality that confronts them. The natural response to this dissonance is to try reducing it by changing one's behavior or beliefs. Either option has a cost. To change behavior is to risk relationships, especially with the significant whites in one's life who remain oblivious to any talk about racism. To change one's beliefs is to reject years of socialization and training. Helms writes: "The social pressure from friends and acquaintances to collude, to not notice racism, can be quite powerful."[10]

Additionally, whites who try to change and ally themselves with BIPOC will often find that they are not welcome. As Helms says, "Many Black people will be suspicious of the motives of a person who devotes so much attention to helping Blacks rather than changing whites."[11] The same could be said of other BIPOC. Thus, white people seeking to change can find themselves feeling ostracized by their white peers and distrusted by the BIPOC. Like my young friend mentioned above, they are stuck in a place of guilt, loneliness and powerlessness.

Collective Guilt

Because whites tend to think of themselves as individuals rather than part of a racialized group, a common reaction to the experience of guilt is to deny one's role in past events and responsibility to correct them. White people will say things like: "I never owned slaves," "I don't use racial slurs" and "Some of my best friends are Black (Latino, Native American etc.)." In their minds, because they themselves did not do something overtly racist, they are not guilty of racism. They will say: "I have friends who are racist, but I'm not," "How can I be racist, there are no BIPOC who live in my community" and "What happened to that Black (Latino, Chinese, etc.) person is terrible, but I had nothing to do with it." Though they see evidence of racism, they distance themselves from it as if they are not connected in any way. They fail to ask the crucial question: "Why?" Why is it okay for a friend or family to use racist language? Why is it that there are no BIPOC in one's community? In what ways are there indirect benefits to whites when BIPOC are being disproportionately harassed or unequally treated? Moreover, as discussed in Chapter 7, because racism has generally become less overt since the Civil Rights Movement, it's convenient for whites to exempt themselves simply because they don't act or speak in overtly racist ways. But as in Chapter 4, simply claiming not to be racist still means that one is racist. One is either racist or anti-racist; there is no middle ground.

Whites generally don't see themselves as a racial group. By contrast, BIPOC learn early in their lives that they are regarded as such. By referencing the impact of history or present societal policies and practices of BIPOC, whites' individualistic worldview is challenged. Tatum says it well: "Understanding racism as a system of advantage that structurally benefits Whites and disadvantages people of color on the basis of group membership threatens not only beliefs about society, but also beliefs about one's own accomplishments."[12] Here Tatum is not only calling for an acceptance of personal guilt, but also collective white guilt for all that has happened in the past as well as the continuing effects of that history, including institutionalized racism in the present.

When confronted with feelings of collective guilt, many whites will revert to their individualistic focus and reject the idea that they share responsibility for historic and systemic racism with other whites.[13] However, when whites begin to grasp that they are part of a racialized group, this awareness can be quite disorienting and add to the personal sense of guilt they may already be experiencing. While this may lead some whites to reject and withdraw, still others are moved to action designed to correct past injustices and work toward greater racial equality and justice.

Guilt Leading to Shame

Sometimes feelings of guilt can become feelings of shame. While clearly related, there are distinct differences; according to Brene Brown, an expert on the psychology of shame, guilt is feeling badly for something *we have done*, whereas shame is feeling badly about *who we are*.[14] The message shame gives is: "I am not worthy or good enough for love, belonging or connection. I'm unlovable. I don't belong."[15] While guilt can often motivate people to work for constructive change in their lives, shame cripples them to the point that they not only don't seek to make changes in their ways of living, they don't think it's possible.

Generally speaking, while whites don't live with a conscious sense of guilt for racism in American culture, Thandeka[16] believes that shame plays a central role in white culture. Similarly, Baldwin[17] comments that white people "found the color of my skin inhibitory." He found that his very presence in groups of white people created defensiveness in them, arising from this deep, unacknowledged shame. Awareness of racist words and actions by significant people in one's youth, such as parents, grandparents, coaches or teachers, gets repressed so one can continue to view these authority figures in a positive light. However, witnessing an incident of racism or being challenged by a BIPOC can bring those feelings of shame to the surface and paralyze people into not knowing what to say or do, nor how to escape the deep pain in their body.

Perhaps the most salient expression of white shame is rejecting one's racial identity as white and wishing to be Black, Brown or some other. Multicultural education expert Dr. Gary Howard, who is white, early in his career worked with African American youth in New Haven, Connecticut. Describing his struggles during that time, he writes:

I had entered a period of rejecting my racial identity. I had learned what it meant to be white in America and I did not want to have anything to do with it. I had broken the seal of my own cultural encapsulation, blown away many of the old images and did not want to be identified with white people anymore. I had opened the door on understanding my own complicity, privilege and racism, and wanted to put this in the face of other white people who had not yet paid their dues. I wanted to be different, not one of them.[18]

Howard eventually moved on from this point in young adulthood to be a leading advocate for whites in education to understand racism and its impact on their students of color. Nonetheless, it's poignant to see how, at a critical time in his life, he felt shame because he was white.[19]

Denying one's racial identity and seeking to embrace another is not only impossible, it's also deceptive to oneself and others. Rachel Dolezal, the former president of the NAACP's Spokane chapter, found this out in a painfully public way. A white woman, she represented herself as an African American for years. In 2015, her family revealed that she had been born white and posing as Black. Dolezal was ousted from her NAACP post and related positions. While some of her former colleagues praised her activism, the general response from the African American community was negative. Even though Dolezal claimed to be "trans-racial," she was not able to escape the perception and reality that she is white.[20]

While I don't know if Dolezal's attempt to "become Black" arose out of shame, her story makes clear that racial constructs in U.S. culture are so clearly fixed that one cannot become something else. That is why white shame can leave one feeling powerless and helpless to make a difference.

Neurotic Guilt and Denial

Sometimes a person's encounter with information or another person is so compelling, the pain of this new awareness can be emotionally and cognitively overwhelming. Instead, the person moves into denial. Hitchcock calls this denial "neurotic guilt" or "a neurotic reaction to guilt."[21] The goal of denial is to block any experience of guilt in favor of maintaining what he calls "the myth of white innocence," the story whites tell themselves that, despite some bumps along the way, the history of whites in America is largely glorious and free of the gross atrocities on which BIPOC and antiracist whites seem to focus. The motto of Republicans in the 2016 election to "Make America Great Again" was a perfect example of white denial. It assumes there was a time when people of all races got along and there was not injustice or inequity. Neurotic guilt and denial seek to minimize past wrongs and propose simplistic idealistic solutions to the complex dynamics of racial injustice. Instead of addressing those, white deniers "blame the victim" by denigrating their families and culture, and characterizing their concerns as empty complaints.

Daniel Hill, a Chicago pastor, describes an experience when he witnessed a clear miscarriage of racial justice. Rather than speaking up or acting, he describes what happened: "Instead I went on an active search for a way to cope with the tidal wave of emotions aroused by that too-close-for-comfort encounter with racism and I exercised my privilege. I chose to walk away."[22] Reflecting later on that experience, Hill realized that he had chosen to exercise the option of white denial. Describing why he reacted as he did, "the encounter shook the whole foundation of my worldview.... I felt shaken to the bone."[23]

An extreme form of denial is to minimize the history of racial oppression in the United States. More than once I have been asked: "Didn't we have a Civil Rights Movement that gave Black people greater freedom? Isn't all that racism stuff just a thing of the past?" A common response will be to try teaching people information they don't know. However, most who deny the history of racism are not looking to be taught; they are reacting emotionally, seeking to deflect and protect their self-image. Facts and figures alone cannot overcome denial.[24]

Such denial among white Americans is critical to a white sense of normalcy, privilege and superiority. One doesn't have to vocally espouse white supremacy; whites are socialized to believe they are the norm for decency, honesty and doing what's right. White denial protects this false image of white innocence and is a critical dimension of white culture. One sees this collective denial in the way American history is described in public-school textbooks. The history of African slavery, Native American genocide and other ethnic oppressions are given only token mention, if at all. Hill comments: "The depth of denial grips our nation as a whole. It doesn't seem to matter how much exposure white America has to racial injustice or how many encounters we have with systemic inequality; we can't seem to snap out of our collective slumber and admit the fault in our foundations."[25]

What Baldwin wrote over 50 years ago is still true:

> The American situation is peculiar and it may be without precedent in the world. No curtain under heaven is heavier than that curtain of guilt and lies behind which Americans hide. That curtain may prove to be more deadly to the lives of human beings than that Iron Curtain of which we speak so much and know so little."[26]

That curtain is white denial and, as Baldwin suggests, it's killing all who live in it.

Responding to White Guilt

So how do we respond to white people who confess or exhibit signs of white guilt and shame? The place to start is to recognize and acknowledge our own histories with guilt and shame. For BIPOC, that history can involve struggles early in life by not accepting one's own racial identity and skin color. Kendi describes at length his own racism against other African Americans and struggle to accept his racial identity.[27] For white people, that history involves many of the same experiences of discomfort, guilt and rejection of one's self and significant others described in this chapter. Howard, whose rejection of his whiteness is described above, goes on to relay his struggles as an assistant minister, venting his wrath on other white people "rejecting my own whiteness and confronting other White people with theirs."[28] He then went to teach 13- and 14-year-olds in rural Washington and came to realize that his students had been socialized to be blinded to the impact of whiteness and racism in their lives. Coming out of that, coupled with his earlier experiences in New Haven, Howard emerged with a greater appreciation for the way racism permeates every dimension and institution of U.S. society. He went back to school and wrote a thesis on multicultural education, and began to develop materials to assist teachers to develop strategies for teaching about racial and cultural diversity.[29]

Kendi describes how facing up to having cancer helped him make sense of the dynamics of racism. He came to realize that coming to terms with his cancer and doing things suggested to him by his doctors helped him to overcome it.[30] Dealing with racism is much the same way. He writes that "the heartbeat of racism is denial, the heartbeat of antiracism is confession."[31]

Without reflection and owning up to one's racism and struggles with guilt, a person is not able to appreciate the power that guilt, shame and denial can have. Without personal awareness, people can easily fall prey to one of two tendencies. Either they will be tempted to pile on the abuse, venting their anger (much like Howard did) and intensifying the sense of personal guilt and powerlessness, or they will be tempted to go easy on the other person seeking to minimize his or her discomfort and sense of responsibility. This tendency is especially true with whites talking with whites. Without owning up to our experiences with guilt, we can feel so uncomfortable with other people's guilt that we seek to let them and ourselves off the hook. As mentioned earlier, white people need to do our own work when it comes to racism, which involves allowing people to feel their discomfort even as we stay with them in the midst of it.

Guilt as a Motivator for Change

In the introduction to this chapter, I mentioned a young man in a work-shop who confessed his guilt and powerlessness and wondered how he could work against racism without feeling so awful. I took the young man's statement at face value. I could see he was in emotional pain and took a moment to formulate my response, replying: "You are right where you need to be." I went on to affirm him and his desire to change his actions. I then said that we cannot authentically deal with racism in our lives and society without struggle. Any sort of significant change in life entails discomfort and difficulty; coming to terms with the prevalence of racism in ourselves and others is doubly so.

Central to the stage of disintegration in Janet Helms' model of white antiracist identity development is the experience of both personal and collective guilt.[32] Guilt is an effective motivator for people to change. So despite the discomfort guilt brings, it's a good thing. What one wants to do is to affirm the person, with encouragement to move through the guilt to constructive action. This involves a six-step process.

First, we need to affirm people for their willingness to consider the reality of racism in their lives and remind them that, despite the pain and discomfort they feel, they are in the right place. We need to make clear that they are not some horrible person, that all of us swim in a societal sea of racism. We need to emphasize that we don't judge them and that we ourselves have struggled with guilt.

Second, we should ask questions that invite them to explore their feelings around issues of race. What are they feeling and what is it that prompted them to feel that way? If there was a particular incident, media event or conversation that engendered the feeling, what happened or what was said, and what prompted the feeling of guilt? Now that they have an opportunity to reflect on the experience, what do they think was going on within them?

Third, we need to tell our story of how we confronted our own guilt. What did we learn about ourselves, upbringing and surroundings through that experience? We need to let them know that guilt is a necessary if painful reminder of the work we still need to do in our lives.

Fourth, we should ask how their guilt helps them understand themselves more fully and the impact racism has on them. What would they like to do next? This step should be handled sensitively with an awareness of just how much individuals are willing to take on. Some options we can offer might include books or videos that can give them a deeper understanding of what racism is. We can introduce them to other white people or groups we are part of where people openly discuss their personal struggles with racism, grapple with what it means to be white, and how to talk with friends and family who don't share their perspectives. If they are not already in social groups that are racially and culturally diverse, we can invite them to join us some of those gatherings.

Fifth, we need to address the fear of hurting others or making mistakes in dealing with BIPOC. We should ask if they have any fears about become involved in antiracist work and allow them to talk about those fears, which need to be acknowledged. They may face rejection from white friends and family members. They may fear saying or doing something that offends a BIPOC. All too often, people on all sides of this issue are quick to condemn and that can be hurtful. Whites, even those who seek to work against racism, are frequently more quick to judge and get angry than listen and affirm when race and racism are discussed.

Finally, we need to warn them that there is tremendous internal and external pressure to simply withdraw from the whole issue and try to hide from it. Helms calls this the reintegration stage, where the white person withdraws from BIPOC and experiences and people who might suggest they are racist and need to change. We will look at this phase more fully in the next chapter. Part of the way we counteract the temptation to withdraw is to gently yet persistently urge the person to continue exploring race-related issues. Where possible, we can ask them to reflect on things like the police shootings of Black and Brown people, the inequities between prison sentences between whites and BIPOC who have committed the same crimes, and why relatively few BIPOC live in predominantly white communities. Such questions have complex answers, but their purpose is to call attention to the many expressions of racism all around us every time that can be denied.

Tatum, commenting on Helms' positive white racial-identity model, points out that racial awareness and identity development is not a linear process; it's more cyclical, where people return to stages again and again.[33] I can personally attest to that. Even though I have intentionally worked on my attitudes, values and emotions, and actively engage in solidarity with BIPOC in many antiracist efforts, I still get tripped up in my own guilt. I do or say things regardless of their intention that cause real harm to BIPOC. In those moments, I have to walk myself through the steps I have outlined here. In the same way, we need to let people know that dealing with racism in ourselves and others in our society is a long and arduous project, and that feelings like guilt may come back around. We just get better at learning from it.

Notes on Shame and Denial

While the six-step process outlined above can also be used with people experiencing shame or expressing denial, these can create barriers to even having the conversation in the first place. So what can we do?

Responding to Shame

When it comes to shame, we need to remember the difference between that and guilt. We should point out that though the person might have done or said something that led to feeling ashamed, ultimately the words or actions and not the person's self-worth are at stake. I remember when—in a Race and Ethnic Relations class—I said something in jest without thinking, which deeply hurt two students of color I greatly respected. Though I apologized and sought to make amends, for several weeks I was immersed in feelings of shame anytime I thought of the incident or the people involved. My shame was rooted in the false idea that to be antiracist meant I would never do or say anything that was offensive or hurtful to BIPOC. I had to come to terms with the fact that, no matter how hard I try, I will do and say things that are hurtful. I will let moments pass when I should have said or done something. I had to come to terms that I am a flawed person who will make mistakes, from which I must learn.

Responding to people experiencing shame requires that we spend a great deal more time and effort in Step 1 affirming their concern about doing or saying something racist, but also assuring them they are not alone. When white people begin to get sensitized to the reality of racism, it can be very crushing and they need to be affirmed that they are not the only ones who made those mistakes.[34]

Denial

Responding to denial is more problematic because such an individual has already put up psychological defenses. Baldwin, speaking of the white people he knew, wrote that they had "a really dazzling ingenuity, a tireless agility ... perpetually defending themselves against charges [of racism]."[35] Denial is a common response that white people make when their assumptions, words and behaviors are challenged as being racist. In their minds, denial exempts them from the accusation. They may hold assumptions such as racism is merely personal prejudice or that racism only occurs when a person intentionally acts in a discriminatory way or reserves the right to decide who is or is not racist.[36]

When we encounter people in denial, the best approach I have found is to ask and probe what it is they object to and try to get at their underlying assumptions. I remember one situation where a person denied he exhibited racism because he supported a certain politician of color. Therefore how could he be racist? So I switched gears and asked him where he first learned what racism was. I tried to explore how he had been socialized by the significant figures in his life. My purpose was to get at his assumptions about race to engage in deeper conversation. I did not try to argue if that politician was truly representative of BIPOC, instead seeking to get underneath his claim that such support confirmed that he was not racist. I would like to say that this completely turned the conversation's direction around, but it did not. He shut down. But I had opened a door that I kept open, and every once in a while that friend comes around and we continue the conversation.

All of this is to say that denial requires patience, persistence and grace with the other person. Our willingness to re-engage them is the most potent and effective thing we can do. Many people working toward antiracist ends ask, "Why bother?" We bother because all the civil-rights laws and policies that are passed will only be as effective as we are able to help white people see their value, not only to BIPOC but also other white people. There is a certain percentage of the white population who will never be convinced, but many whites feel caught in a quandary over how much of a problem racism is. These are the people we are trying to reach, who with consistent and persistent engagement can be led to investigate the value of examining the impact that racism has had on their lives.

Conclusion

White guilt is a sign of the fragility of white people around issues of race.[37] People of European descent have had the privileged and power position in the world for centuries. Since 1619 in this country, whites have passed laws, built an economy, created an educational system, redlined BIPOC (particularly African Americans) into certain geographical areas, and so much more that assures they have greater access to resources and opportunities than BIPOC. This complex system of white supremacy has surrounded them in such a way that they don't see what their peers of color have to contend with every day of their lives. Like overly protected children, many whites are unprepared to come to terms with the system that has favored them and deeply oppressed others. When they begin to see those disparities, this is where guilt, shame and denial can arise.

Whites grappling with these emotions must be handled firmly but gently, challenged to probe their sources of guilt and shame and to reflect on the reasons for their denial when the evidence is so clear. The weight of history may make whites feel guilty, but the ultimate goal is that they take responsibility for correcting the inequities and systemic forces that caused them. As devastating as guilt may seem, racial-identity development theories remind us that guilt is a positive first step toward helping white people own their part in our racist society, and work alongside BIPOC to bring about the changes needed.

Fears, Tears and Anger

The courageous have fears that cowards never know.
— Stanley Hauerwas

Fear: The Root of Racism

When I was growing up, I learned that in polite, middle-class white society, when attending a social event, people were to avoid talking about religion and politics. I was told that those topics could be inherently divisive and, if one was not careful, they might stir up unnecessary controversy in an otherwise friendly setting. In today's polarized political climate (which is often exacerbated by some religious views), this advice still holds some merit. However, in my experience there is a topic even more divisive: race. On more than one occasion I have found that when the conversation turns even to the words "race" or "racism," it quickly moves to a more benign subject. Even in a setting where it's clearly an appropriate topic, such as in my course Race and Ethnic Relations, white people have to be gently coaxed to share their thoughts.

In my experience, the key reason for this hesitancy is white fear. Kendi[1] contends that the basis of racism is denial and Banks asserts that anger is at the foundation of contemporary racism, but I believe it's fear.[2] As Howard states, "Fear is the classic White American reaction to any intrusion into our cultural capsule."[3] He goes on to describe how in high school a white male friend invited him to join a double date with his Black girlfriend and one of her Black friends. Despite no apparent external threats, Howard confessed that his first response was fear. He was being invited to step outside the prescribed norms of his white habitus. Despite the assurances of his white friend, Howard was flooded with internal questions like, "What will happen to me? Will I be safe? What will other white people think of me? ... Will I survive?"[4] Like Howard, I confess that I, too, have found myself experiencing fear when entering an otherwise benign and welcoming space where BIPOC are in the majority. More often than not, that fear has been reinforced by my white friends, family members and generally the way I was raised.

However, even in situations where the white person has a clear advantage, fear is often cited as a reason for extreme action. George Zimmerman defended his murder of Trayvon Martin by saying that he felt threatened by the younger Martin.[5] Joe Glaser killed former New York Jets running back Joe McKnight because he could not believe a Black man could be law abiding.[6] In Ferguson, Missouri, police officer Darrin Wilson shot unarmed Michael Brown 12 times, hitting his body six times because he felt threatened.[7] Two Sacramento, California, police officers shot Stephon Clark 20 times when he raised his hands because they believed he had a gun, when all he had was a cellphone.[8] In all of these cases and many more like them, the white shooters justified their action because of fear and the courts exonerated them on that basis. Had the shooters been Black and the victims white, one can be certain that such leniency would not have been proffered.

In a society where whiteness defines social norms and institutions certify those norms, their inviolability is unquestioned. However, when those same norms are challenged, white people experience a sense of disequilibrium. For the white people involved, "there is an interruption to that which is familiar and taken for granted" and one experiences fear and its many cognates—hurt, victimization, powerlessness, angst and anger.[9]

The Sources of White Fear

Where does this fear come from? What is its basis? And how is that fear expressed?

Fear, like the racism it creates, is not based on actual threats or reasons to be frightened, and therefore one must look to the emotional terrain of white history and identity for insight. White fear finds its genesis in the history of white oppression, inhuman and subhuman images of BIPOC through the ages, challenges to white identity norms, demographic changes and fear of the unknown.

History of White Oppression

As discussed in Chapter 5, we are all products of our history, but what most whites know and celebrate is the master narrative of European exploration and expansionism. Whites know little of the history or experience of BIPOC in the American narrative, and what they do know has been sanitized and minimized. White fear ultimately arises out of the history of white oppression and genocide that has been hidden or ignored in the master narrative. Recent scholarship has begun to revise the American historical account to include the contributions of indigenous peoples, enslaved Africans, dispossessed Mexicans, exploited Asians and other underrepresented ethnic groups. As a result, the narrative of European exploration, westward expansion and economic advancement has been challenged and revised to include these other perspectives. In the process, white brutality and manipulation have been laid bare and critiqued. Thus for the first time many white Americans are being exposed to the less honorable and more sordid aspects of their American story.

However, even if that story was not being lifted up, the impact of white oppression has produced white-body supremacy trauma.[10] As reviewed in Chapter 4, centuries of white oppression in both Europe and the United States have caused white people to lose touch with their basic humanity, integrity and morality. Instead of coming to terms with their history, whites have gone to great lengths to deny or minimize the brutality of their ancestors and the continuing effects of that brutality. A symptom of that denial is fear.

One of the little-noted aspects of the history of U.S. slavery is how often an increase of violence against the African slaves was a response to fear. For instance, the defeat of an uprising of indentured white servants and African slaves called Bacon's Rebellion in 1676 motivated the landed gentry to create social and economic barriers between poor whites and the African slaves who worked beside them in the fields.[11] In 1791, the slave rebellion on the island of Haiti resulted in the abolition of slavery in that colony. White slaveowners in the American South feared that the rebellion would give their slaves hope that they, too, could overthrow their masters. Such fears moved these slaveowners to adopt harsher forms of discipline and punishment, call for tougher laws on the control of human property and stir up greater antipathy toward those calling for slavery's abolition.[12] While such actions caused terrible suffering for the African slaves, they also embedded fear in the white psyche. This epigenetic trauma has been passed down to later generations of whites. Thus, contemporary whites experience fear when presented with the opportunity to engage with people of other racial backgrounds, a fear rooted in historic body trauma.

A Legacy of Dehumanization

Along with that racial fear, whites have also inherited a legacy of negative caricatures of BIPOC. Black men have been portrayed as beasts and Black women as hyper-sexual, Hispanics are characterized as drug dealers and murderers, and Native Americans as listless and lazy. These images have been propagated by scientists, politicians and the media well into the early 20th century; many whites have thus come to believe that BIPOC are not only "other," but also subhuman and dangerous. Even when whites don't express adherence to such views, these images are subconsciously embedded in their minds and influence where they go, who they interact with and how they interpret events.

Until the 1950s and 1960s and the Civil Rights Movement, most white Americans subscribed explicitly and implicitly to the notion that BIPOC were inferior to white people and should therefore should not have access to the same rights as whites. However, in the post-civil-rights era, most whites no longer subscribe to the overt dehumanization of BIPOC. Rather, they hold what Banks calls "symbolic racism" or "racial resentment."[13] Instead of considering BIPOC as inferior and therefore undeserving, racial resentment blames BIPOC for not working hard enough, being dishonest, and responsible for their own lack of success. This view denies the history that has created the inequality while rejecting any efforts to undo it and level the playing field. So either by outright bigotry or racial resentment, the dominant white establishment keeps BIPOC as a group at an emotional, social and economic distance.

Challenging White identity

In Chapter 3 in talking about white privilege and identity, I noted that most white people in the United States consider their education, up-bringing and value system to be the standard and norm for all people regardless of race, culture or economic standing. I also noted that there is a rise in awareness of past injustices done to BIPOC and whites are becoming aware of their whiteness for the first time. Because of their lack of connection to personal and ancestral white history, they don't see themselves in any way culpable or responsible for the injustices and inequities resulting from that history. While they may espouse support for integrated schools and neighborhoods, the reality is that neighborhoods and school districts are as segregated today as they were in 1954 when the Supreme Court ordered schools desegregated.[14] Moreover, the quality of education for students of color lags far beyond the typical predominantly white school district.

This growing awareness of inequities causes an imbalance of identity. DiAngelo writes: "White equilibrium is a cocoon of racial comfort, centrality, superiority, entitlement, racial apathy and obliviousness all rooted in an identity of being good people free of racism. Challenging the cocoon throws off [whites'] racial balance. Because being racially off balance is so rare, [whites] have not had to build the capacity to sustain the discomfort."[15] The feeling of confusion and powerlessness that comes with that imbalance is very threatening, resulting in fear, insecurity and anxiety.

The Challenge of Demographic Changes

Demographic research points clearly to a changing racial/ethnic make-up of American society. If birth and death rates continue on their current trajectory, by the early 2040s white people will make up less than 50% of the population of the United States, which will be a conglomerate of various racial/ethnic groups. This news should be a strong motivation for whites to prepare for the day they are no longer the majority. Instead, for many whites these trends are a source of great fear and anxiety based not only on a decline in white dominance but also an expectation that BIPOC will demand and take more resources, thus lowering the general standard of living among whites.

This fear of demographic changes was clearly articulated by Pat Buchanan, a recognized conservative cultural critic and former speechwriter for President Richard Nixon. During the 2016 presidential campaign, Buchanan actively supported the candidacy of Donald Trump. In an interview on National Public Radio, he was quoted as saying, "If we don't get control of our borders, by 2050 Americans of European descent will be a minority in the nation their ancestors built."[16] Implied in that statement is the assumption that a U.S. not dominated and controlled by white people is a disaster. Like Buchanan, many white nationalist organizations supported Donald Trump for president because they saw him as a candidate who shared their fear of an America not controlled by whites. Since becoming president, Trump has played on that fear in his diatribes against Muslim Americans, undocumented immigrants and residents of African countries. According to some researchers, that fear of demographic decline has an impact on white social and political attitudes due to this perceived existential threat.[17]

The Unknown

Many whites are not aware and connected to the full history of the U.S., and have been ill-prepared to understand and appreciate people of different races and ethnicities. In essence, many whites don't know what they don't know. Even among those whites who aspire to be antiracist and allies to BIPOC, talking about racism can be daunting. Conversations about racism can leave them feeling blamed, shamed, attacked and victimized.[18]

I have witnessed this fear of the unknown in my students and in social situations. Well-meaning whites have expressed to me that they "don't know what to say" when around BIPOC. They are afraid of saying something wrong or even hurtful. They fear being labeled racist without knowing exactly why. I myself can relate to that fear. Even though I have taught many courses and attended numerous antiracism workshops, I often experience that fear of saying something that will be perceived in a way that is less than favorable. I also have come to know that as a middle-aged, educated white male, I am often perceived by BIPOC whom I have never met as someone who is clueless when it comes to racial dynamics. Being misperceived that way makes me afraid as well. This fear of the unknown, of saying or doing something perceived as racist, can be paralyzing.

Expressions of Fear

Whether it's a result of trauma passed down from ancestors, the influence of negative images of BIPOC, a challenge to exalted white identity, a fear of demographic changes or just not knowing what to say or do, white fear is real and pervasive. How that fear is expressed is varied, but three particular types of responses tend to dominate. When whites experience racial fear or stress, they either withdraw, cry or get angry.

Withdrawal

When an individual feels threatened, regardless if that threat is physical or emotional, the intrinsic biological response is either fight, flight or freeze. When it comes to white fear, withdrawal or avoidance is a common response to encounters with racism; in Chapter 2 I referred to this as aversive racism.

Earlier in this chapter, I shared that often in predominantly white social settings people change the subject when the topic of race is broached. In mixed-race settings, this avoidance is a defensive maneuver against being called a racist. For many whites, there are social taboos against talking about race; they see the issue in simplistic good/bad terms. Some whites harbor unacknowledged fears of BIPOC, while they like to think of themselves as open-minded, objective and fair. The entire purpose of avoidance is to limit racial stress and maintain the white person's belief that he or she is a good person. By not engaging the topic or interacting with BIPOC in a meaningful way, white people believe they can avoid the charge of being racist.[19]

However, while avoidance may seem a way of protecting oneself from the charge of racism, the effect of avoidance on BIPOC is quite different. The choice not to engage the issue of racism or to interact with BIPOC about race reinforces the historical and social power that whites have to not consider the experiences, needs or desires of BIPOC. White avoidance sends the message that the daily confrontations BIPOC have in U.S. society are of no consequence and don't need to be addressed. Even if a white person avoids the topic of racism because of fear, the message conveyed is "BIPOC, your struggles for fairness and justice don't matter. It's not something that I as a white person need to address." Thus, while avoidance is the white person's strategy for self-protection, it actually widens the gap of understanding and relationship.

Tears

In the experience of many BIPOC, as well as facilitators of antiracism trainings, the expressions of fear tend to be gender-based. White men tend to respond in anger and defensiveness, whereas white women tend to respond with tears. If withdrawal is a flight response to white fear, tears are a freeze response, an expression of powerlessness and being overwhelmed.

Sarita Srivastava[20] studied feminist social-justice organizations in Toronto, Canada. She looked at how the women in those organizations processed their emotions in conversations about racism, noting that very often when the issue of race was raised, it was met with emotional resistance to the topic and led to women expressing their fear in tears. When these women engaged in antiracism discussions, the white participants often spoke "in an emotional manner about their commitment, hope, solidarity, complicity, guilt, lack of complicity, failure to understand, disbelief and hurt that they have been accused; tears [were] the most commonly described reaction."[21]

While tears are natural expressions of human emotion, they have much broader social and political impact. Tears have the effect of dismissing the real pain and struggles faced by BIPOC. When white women cry in conversations about race, all too often the focus of the conversation shifts from the pain and struggle to overcome racism to sympathy for the white woman crying. DiAngelo says that "well-meaning white women crying in cross-racial interactions is one of the most pernicious enactments of white fragility."[22] If tears are a result of some honest feedback on the individual's words or actions being racist, they reinforce the woman's privilege to have her needs met before those of BIPOC in the room. In an effort to defend the white woman who may feel hurt, other whites will often criticize BIPOC for being too harsh, direct and honest about how they perceive their white peers. In essence, BIPOC are being asked to suppress their needs and opinions in deference to an aggrieved white person. Though not necessarily intended, tears serve the purpose of dismissing the views of BIPOC and undermining their concerns. While the tears may be genuine, they serve the purpose of reinforcing rather than challenging white supremacy. Thus it's important for white people, especially white women, to be aware of the impact their tears may have on others.

Anger

Anger is the fight response to white fear and tends to be a response more often had by men. Expressions of anger tend to take the form of outrage, defensiveness and aggression. At the root of the response is often the feeling of "How dare you suggest that I could have done or said something racist?" Because white men's fear tends to focus on the loss of power and privilege, responding with anger is a way of seeking to regain that power.

In his book, *Angry White Men*, sociologist Michael Kimmel interviewed white men across the United States about why they were angry.[23] He writes: "They are America's angry white men. Actually, one might say simply they're just America's white men—they just happen to be angrier than ever before in our recent history."[24] He interviewed working-class, middle-class and well-to-do men from all sectors of the nation. When asked why they were angry, they said they were upset about not being able to achieve what their parents and grandparents had done before them. They were angry about the increased emphasis on gender and race as issues that they were being asked to care about. They felt like the American Dream they believed in and may have fought to preserve in the military is slipping away. They listened to talk-radio hosts like Rush Limbaugh, who validated and stoked their anger. The men Kimmel interviewed were the people whose fear and anger Donald Trump tapped into to win the 2016 presidential election. And while they may cite a range of reasons for their outrage, Kimmel states that the issue underlying everything he heard is a loss of their "culturally bankrupt entitlement."[25]

Despite enjoying advantages and privileges unavailable to other racial and ethnic groups in society, white people often see any advances or progress toward equal access as a threat. While they may espouse a desire for equal rights and belief in equality across all racial and ethnic groups, those ideals and values can quickly devolve into anger when it's believed that the advancement of the "other" may be at their expense.[26] That fear-based anger is felt by conservatives, moderates and liberals alike; it's not reserved for one political group.

Responding to Fear

When white fear manifests itself in various expressions of withdrawal, tears or anger, how are we to respond? How can we help white people gain a deeper understanding of the sources of their misplaced fear? Even more, how can we help move people from fear to openness, and to understanding themselves and the BIPOC in their lives?

The Irrationality of Fear and Anger

Fear and the racism it produces are not rational. Rarely can one be reasoned out of their fear. Reactions to fear are not logical; they are emotional. When the African American community of Ferguson protested the shooting of Michael Brown, sales of firearms to white people in Missouri skyrocketed.[27] When marches in support of Black Lives Matter began happening all over the country, white people started putting signs on their laws with messages of "Blue Lives Matter" and "All Lives Matter." Most white Americans did not stop to consider why there were protests and marches in response to the Ferguson shooting. Instead, they were driven by their fear to protect themselves from a perceived threat of African American retaliation. By and large, the protestors were not seeking vengeance; rather, they looked for recognition and acknowledgement of the perilous existence of Black and Brown people in the United States today. But white people weren't listening or even seeking to understand.

This response of irrational fear sometimes morphs into anger. In the aftermath of George Floyd's death, the chant "Black Lives Matter" has taken on new poignancy. White people, especially young white adults, have joined the marches and demonstrations, making clear that the Black

Lives Matter movement has significant white support. This has led to white fear leading to more intense anger.

In early August 2020, a Black Lives Matter march in a working-class suburb of Philadelphia began as a peaceful walk a little over a mile to the local police station. While walking, they chanted "Black Lives Matter" and "Who's street? Our street?" Two pickup trucks passed them spewing sooty exhaust smoke on the walkers. Others, mostly white men, jeered at them from the sidewalks. When they arrived at the police station, the marchers were met by a group of white men on motorcycles who began pushing and shoving. One woman had a flag ripped from her hands. The counter-protestors shouted, "All Lives Matter." The confrontation became a shouting match and police had to separate the two groups. Eventually, one of the leaders of the march thanked everyone for marching and they dispersed.

When interviewed, the leader said, "We came for a peaceful demonstration and we're going to stay on that note."[28] Ironically, the counter-protestors that day saw the simple presence of marchers as a threat asking for a fight.

While white fear is always present, it becomes most evident after a public and tragic incident like the shooting of Michael Brown or Trayvon Martin or George Floyd or Jacob Blake that sparks a massive response. Precipitating incidents may be national in scope like the Brown and Floyd cases, or they may be local. On such occasions, Black and Brown anger becomes undeniably apparent and white fear spikes; it's during such times when one has the greatest opportunity to address white fear. And because it does little good attempting to reason or explain people out of their fear, one must start by acknowledging the fear itself.

Acknowledging Fear

Whether the fear manifests as withdrawal, tears, anger or some combination of these, it's important to acknowledge how difficult it is to deal with issues around race and racism, and that white people's fear (however misguided we may think it is) is real. It does no good to tell people that there is no reason to be afraid, hurt or angry, if that is what they are feeling. They may even deny feeling anything. So one should start with their reaction. Why did they back away? What prompted the tears? What brought on the anger? And then it helps to follow up by asking them what has prompted that reaction in the past.

I once had an adult student who was very hesitant to talk about race in a course where that was a major subject. Nonetheless, it became evident that he held strong animosity toward BIPOC. In the final paper for the course, he wrote about an experience when he was driving with his family and a march comprised mostly of African Americans surrounded his car. People were shouting, not at him but about the cause that prompted the march. Nonetheless, the man was scared for his family's safety. The marchers went around his car and neither hurt it nor threatened his family, but it clearly terrified him. Unfortunately, I never saw that student again and so had no opportunity to speak with him. Had I done so, I would have started by asking him to retell that story. Then I would have asked if he knew about what the marchers were protesting or for what they were advocating. But before I could get him to think about the racial issues involved, I would have had to start with his experience.

It's highly likely that my former student experienced trauma in having his family surrounded by the marchers. Menakem[29] has worked with both Blacks and whites dealing with their racial trauma and states: "Changing the world begins with our bodies."[30] Before we can have a reasonable conversation with fearful and/or traumatized white people, we must acknowledge what is going on in their white bodies. He goes on to say that when whites experience race-based trauma, their reasoning often goes to "Something is wrong with African Americans" (or Hispanics, Native Americans, immigrants, Muslims, etc.).[31] Instead of asking, "What is wrong with me?" when the trauma revolves around race, whites project their fear onto the racial other. After white people acknowledge their fear, they must own it; otherwise, they will end up like my former student: angry and resistant to any interaction with BIPOC.

Racial Stress and Storytelling

Howard Stevenson,[32] a clinical psychologist and professor of applied psychology at the University of Pennsylvania, has spent his career working with young men of color, helping them manage what he refers to as racial stress. He describes it as that experience of anxiety and tension that often occurs when whites and BIPOC interact in the course of their daily lives. Stevenson's work involves helping young men of color understand this, especially with external authority figures like police officers and teachers, and to manage their stress in ways that keep get them from getting hurt or even killed. For many Black and Brown people, especially young ones, these are basic survival skills in a culture that continues to distrust and oppress them. Yet Stevenson recognizes that this stress is also experienced by white people who encounter BIPOC.

To enable young BIPOC to effectively manage their racial stress, Stevenson helps identify the racial dynamics in a situation by engaging in personal storytelling. In a similar way, I suggest that when whites are experiencing racial fear, they should be encouraged to tell the story of what prompted their fear reaction in a process that Stevenson calls "racial recasting," which involves asking a series of questions related to the story.[33] While he poses these questions for African Americans, I have adapted them to talk with white people about interracial encounters when they experience feelings of fear, anger or tears:

- When you were in this racial encounter, what were you thinking? What were you feeling?
- In what ways was this like other racial encounters you have had? How did you respond to those previous experiences?
- Growing up, how were you taught to handle these kind of situations with Black people? With Latinx people? Asians? Native Americans?
- What do you notice in other white people who get upset about racial issues, conflict or politics?
- When you go into mixed-race settings, what are the assumptions you make about how Blacks/Latinx/Asians/Native Americans will react or view you? What assumptions do you make about them?
- Are there ways your previous training and assumptions may have contributed to how you react?

- Now that you have had an opportunity to think about it, are there ways you might have handled yourself in such situations differently?

The point of asking people to tell their story and then analyze it with these sorts of questions is twofold. First, it helps them move out of just focusing on their emotions to analyzing them. Second, by retelling a story, people hear themselves say things that cause them to reflect more deeply on why they reacted the way they did. Stevenson calls this Racial Encounter Awareness. He observes: "Through storytelling, individuals can learn how to observe emotional and physiological reactions to an event before and after the event occurs. In one's story there exists the freedom to explore challenges and successes in the encounter."[34]

When dealing with a white person who is angry, one must assure his or her safety, asking: Is this anger going to turn physically or verbally violent, such that I must take protective measures? Is the other person's anger generating a fight/flight/freeze response in me? If I don't perceive a threat, is there a way to engage the other person in a dialogue? So often in situations like that described above, there is a misunderstanding of what is being said. Saying Black lives matter doesn't mean white lives don't matter; it just means that Black lives matter as well. Only as people begin to process their emotions, their mind might be open to a new understanding. However, such a meeting of minds is sometimes not possible, especially when rage and uncontrolled anger are present. In such moments, one must wait for another time to interact.

Unpacking Intent and Impact

One thing that often occurs in racial encounters is the white person may say or do something with relatively good intentions, which is then taken in a negative way by BIPOC. During the 2008 Democratic primary, then-Senator Joe Biden referred to his primary competitor, Barack Obama, this way: "I mean, you got the first mainstream African American who is articulate and bright and clean and a nice-looking guy. I mean, that's a storybook, man."[35] Biden experienced tremendous backlash for this comment from the African American community because, while he may have meant to give Obama a compliment, his comment also implied that, generally speaking, African Americans are not articulate, bright, clean and nice-looking. Biden's *intention* may have been positive, but the *impact* was negative.

In the same way, when white people realize the negative impact of their words, they react in fear by withdrawing and becoming defensive. At such times, it can be helpful to remind them about the intent-impact tension by giving positive and effective feedback. One should help the other person understand how and why the statement may have been misconstrued and show why it may have hurt or offended the BIPOC. The feedback should be concrete and as soon as possible after the incident. Then one can explore how the person could have made his or her point in a non-offensive way. If one happens to be in the room when the statement is made or action is taken, it can be helpful to share how the incident impacted them. The point is not to shame or blame, but to help the person understand why the misunderstanding and hurt occurred, and how they can learn ways to act and speak differently going forward.[36]

The Need for White Courage
In the end, while it's important to acknowledge the fear that white people feel, and help them analyze and learn from their experiences, we must also invite white people to live with the discomfort that often occurs in interracial encounters and to move forward in courage. When I first taught courses on racism, I would start each class by claiming that the classroom was a "safe space." Yet over the years, I realized that I could not guarantee the conversations and interactions on race-based issues and experiences would always feel safe. And so I changed and invited my students to enter a courageous—rather than safe—space.

Courage is moving forward despite our fear. The renowned Christian ethicist Stanley Hauerwas' words are telling: "The courageous have fears that cowards never know." To live courageously, we must face our fears. If people of all different racial and ethnic backgrounds are going to live and work together constructively in this society, we must walk together in courage. And so as we engage the white people in our lives on issues and experiences of race, we must ask them: Do you want to live in fear? Or are you willing to face your fear and, with courage, continue to try working with people who are racially different than you? Only that way will white fear become a footnote rather than a daily reality for many white people in our society.

Uncovering the Lie of Reverse Racism

*Some people are born on third base and go
through life thinking they hit a triple.*

—Barry Switzer

The Job I Did Not Get

Several years ago, I interviewed for an assistant-director position at an educational institution. The man interviewing me, who was my potential supervisor, I knew from my church. So our interaction was friendly and it was clear that I was more than qualified for the job. As our interview came to a close, he confided to me that the institution was looking to hire a BIPOC, so that I should not get my hopes up. At the time I was surprised by his comment; what I now realize is that his comment was a form of white solidarity.[1] I responded that I certainly understood the need for diversity, but I also felt set up to see whoever was offered the job was getting it only because of his or her race.

As it turned out, the position was filled by an African American woman and I took great interest in her qualifications and who she was; she was far more qualified than I. She went on to hold a few other responsible positions at the institution and later left to become president of another organization, where she served successfully. I was grateful that she was as capable and competent as she was, because I realized then and even now how easy it could have been for me to fall into an attitude of reverse racism.

White Privilege and the Charge of Reverse Racism

White people making claims of reverse racism are expressions of white privilege. In Chapter 3 I noted that many, if not most, white people in the United States cringe and get defensive when the topic of white privilege is raised. They often feel like they are being charged with some sort of crime of which they had no knowledge. They feel like their efforts at self-improvement and getting ahead in life socially and economically are somehow undermined and dismissed. They fail to see or acknowledge that the privilege they have is based on the way society's laws and systems function and not simply on their abilities or merit. Privilege is not something white people do, but rather something they were given without their knowledge or consent.

For many whites, especially white men, this creates great tension. Having lived unknowingly with privilege, they find themselves competing with white women and BIPOC in ways they had not encountered before. When organizations, like the one to which I applied, say they are looking to hire a woman or a BIPOC, they are attempting to level a playing field that has long been tilted in the white man's favor. A man's individualistic racial frame prevents him from seeing the large institutional and systemic forces that have previously favored white men.

Data on all areas of social life—intergenerational wealth, health, wages, home ownership, education levels, incarceration rates and more—all reveal that on average whites earn more, amass greater levels of wealth, achieve higher levels of education, reach higher positions in business, live longer and stay healthier than BIPOC.[2] And yet when policies such as affirmative-action initiatives are enacted, whites often claim reverse racism; they believe they are victims of discrimination when BIPOC have been given the same access to opportunities in education or the workplace that they have had for centuries. In recent decades, court cases have even been brought against colleges and universities with affirmative-action plans on the assumption that if the plaintiffs were not white, they would have gained admission to the school of their choice.[3]

Tragically, whites will cry "reverse racism" even in situations where no affirmative-action policies exist. Arizona State professor of education Nolan Cabrera conducted a study of white male students at two different universities. One of the schools was more academically competitive than the other and so all students, including those he interviewed, were held to higher academic standards. At the more competitive school, white male students expressed anger because they believed that their lower social and academic standing in the university was due to its affirmative-action policies, even though they had been discontinued 10 years earlier. Cabrera's insight from this study was that individuals' perception of reverse racism is not based on concrete facts, but rather distorted by emotions such as fear and anger.[4] In a similar manner, in 2016 then-candidate Donald Trump repeatedly claimed that undocumented immigrants and refugees were taking jobs from working-class whites, when there was no empirical evidence to back up that claim. Just the belief of the advancement of BIPOC creates a misperception leading to claims of reverse racism.

The Perspective of History
Legal scholar Stanley Fish points out that the charge of reverse racism only makes sense if whites ignore the history of racism in this country.[5] While there has been great progress in curbing overt expressions of racism in our society, less overt institutional and systemic racism still widely exists. Just because whites have not been made aware of their institutional, systemic and cultural advantages doesn't mean they don't exist. Calling attention to the reality of white privilege challenges whites to rethink their perspectives on opportunities, failures and successes, and realize that their unearned advantages can be quite disorienting.

Since the election of President Barack Obama, there has been a growing sentiment among some white people in the United States that anti-white racism is on the rise. This "myth is predicated on a feeling by many white people that racism against Black people is largely over but racism against white people is on the rise."[6] In a 2011 study of 209 whites and 208 Blacks, researchers found that both groups believed there was a decrease in anti-Black racism from the 1950s to the 2000s. However, the whites found there was a significant increase—over 200%—of anti-white racism in that same period. In fact, they saw anti-white racism higher than anti-Black racism. Blacks, on the other hand, reported they thought that anti-white racism was nearly non-existent.[7]

What About Low-Income Whites?
What complicates the issue is that there is a significant percentage of low-income and working-class whites for whom the American myth of

meritocracy is a false promise. While low-income whites don't have to contend with the barriers of racism, they do face economic discrimination. Although they may have some level of race privilege, it's moderated by economic disparity. Grappling with this paradox, Kendi makes the distinction between racism and racist power. While the skin color of low-income and working-class whites may give them some social advantages, they are not in a position to dictate social and economic policies. On the other hand, racist policy makers (who are almost exclusively white corporate and political leaders) craft policies and practices that maintain their position in society and wealth at the expense of both BIPOC and working-class and low-income whites.[8]

In the 2016 election, Trump capitalized on the angst and fear of the white working class to get elected. With thinly disguised racist slogans like "Make American Great Again" and "Take America Back," he employed the 17th-century tactic of divide and conquer.[9] Trump stoked the fears of working-class whites, suggesting that white poverty was due to the influx of immigrants and BIPOC into the workforce. In reality, low-income whites and BIPOC have far more in common when it comes to their economic struggles. By creating the mirage of reverse racism, he deceived whites into thinking BIPOC were the "problem" and not unjust policies that affected them both. In the 2020 election, Trump used several tactics that appealed to white racial fears. He suggested that low-income people would overrun suburban communities, criticized calls to take down monuments of Confederate generals, dismissed instances of police brutality against Blacks and called Black Lives Matter "a symbol of hate." While including Black and Latinx supporters in the Republican convention, his overall focus was tapping into the grievances of white voters.[10]

Barriers to White Understanding

What is important to note is that charges of reverse racism are not based on any empirical reality, but by a white racial frame[11] accompanied by emotions such as fear, anger and distrust. These serve to block whites from seeing and admitting their racial privilege, thereby causing them to deny and ignore the reality of racial disparity.

The white racial frame creates what Cabrera calls an "epistemology of [white] ignorance," based more on emotion than awareness of the facts.[12] Often white liberals will claim that the racism is due to ignorance and if people were better educated they would not be as racist. Cabrera disagrees. He says that "the challenge becomes breaking down the affective shield that helps insulate white denial."[13] In other words, whites don't make claims of reverse racism because they are uninformed, but rather because they feel threatened and afraid. Thus in addressing perceptions of reverse racism, one cannot simply try to provide more information; one must address the feelings that keep them from seeing reality for what it is.

In addition, as has been previously noted, whites don't generally think of themselves as part of a distinct racial group but as individuals, while they tend to think of Blacks, Latinos, Native Americans and Asians as collective racial and ethnic groups. They fail to recognize the institutional policies and practices that create vast inequities between whites and BIPOC *as groups*. Thus, any response to charges of reverse racism must deal with this perceptual lens distorting their view of reality.

Finally, as mentioned in Chapter 9, white fear of retaliation by BIPOC is rooted in historical body trauma.[14] This epigenetic fear is a barrier to understanding, which is still very much alive today. For instance, following the election of Barack Obama, many whites believed that he favored BIPOC over whites, even though he repeatedly affirmed and acted as the president of *all* Americans and not just some.[15]

Responding to Charges of Reverse Racism

When the topic of reverse racism comes up, it's important to determine the source of the claim being made. Is it due to a personal experience when whites feel they lost an opportunity to a BIPOC, or is it a more general claim that whites are somehow being pushed to the margins, while BIPOC are moving forward? Then it's important to identify from where their information came. What evidence is the person relying on for such a claim? What are the sources? Often it's flimsy because such claims are due more to a false narrative that circulates in some white spaces than hard data. By simply raising questions about that narrative, one should not be surprised that white people feel uncomfortable and hard-pressed to substantiate their claims.

While understanding the source of one's claims about reverse racism is important, at the same time one needs to identify the feelings that lie behind it. Is it fear? Anger? Hurt? Frustration? While BIPOC as a matter of course must learn how to respond to racist actions, words and policies on a regular basis, whites generally have no personal experience to understand what reverse racism actually is. Mistakenly, they can assume their bad feelings are due to some form of discrimination. When it comes to being victimized by racism, white people don't know what they don't know.

Starting the Conversation

In dealing with claims of reverse racism, I start by simply asking: What happened to make you think you have been discriminated against? What was said or done? What feelings do you have about this situation? What makes you think you lost out on an opportunity because you are white? Would you have felt the same way if a white person had been moved ahead of you? What makes you think it's because of race and not something else?

If the claim of reverse racism is more broad and general (for instance when responding to anti-immigrant sentiment), I ask: What makes you say that immigrants are taking American jobs? What are the jobs that white people have lost due to immigrants? Are they jobs Americans are trying to get? Are the immigrants capable of doing the jobs they have? What evidence do you have to back up your claims? When you say immigrants are taking your jobs, how does that make you feel?

The purpose of these opening questions is twofold. First, we gain information about why people think and feel the way they do. Second, we allow them to tell their story and at the same time hear themselves explaining their reasons for thinking and feeling the way they do. For instance, in the example of immigrants taking jobs, people may either realize these are jobs that whites have generally rejected, or those hired are actually quite qualified even though they came from another country. In these conversations, we walk a fine line between honoring people's feelings while raising questions about their claims of discrimination.

Probing Deeper

Having identified the assumptions and reasons of which people think and feel as they do, then it's time to examine them. For instance, we might ask: Whether you agree or not, why do you think the institution (school or workplace) would have an affirmative-action policy? What is the underlying inequity they are attempting to address? If they have no answer, then it's appropriate to talk about the historic and ongoing inequities in education, healthcare, income, job promotions and more based on race. Many whites tend to think such inequities no longer exist, or are due to individual effort rather than systemic racism. There are all sorts of examples from programs like ABC reporter John Quinones' "What Would You Do?" that illustrate ways in which whites routinely are treated more favorably than BIPOC, even if they have the exact same credentials.[16] If one has a personal story, like the one I shared in the introduction to this chapter, it's appropriate to share it in this context. The purpose at this point is to present an alternative perspective to the white racial frame that all advancement and success in life is due to individual merit.

When interacting with whites from low-income or working-class backgrounds, I have even gone on to explain the practice of divide and conquer.[17] The struggle for racial justice is not a zero-sum game and needs to be stressed at every point. In many ways, low-income whites face many of the same barriers to job opportunities due to classism that BIPOC face because of racism. They actually have far more in common and must be wary of politicians and corporate leaders who play on their fears of reverse racism to get their support, while doing little to address their needs and concerns.

Getting Pushback

Initially, the primary goal of such questions and interactions is to cause people to question and reflect on the false narrative they have been given that leads to claims of reverse racism. Because that narrative is so strong and emotionally based, we should expect pushback. Our questions may make people uncomfortable and upset. As a rule, we must not be surprised or get defensive when that pushback comes. We need to approach the conversation seeking their best interest, not trying to prove them wrong.

We don't have to call people racist; our questions could make them feel that is what we are doing. More than once I have been accused of being racist toward white people, in conversations about reverse racism. I respond by agreeing that I am racist, but not in the way they think. I stress that I am trying to work against racism. That usually stops people. It's not a gimmick; I am just trying to communicate that I am not against white people. I am with them and trying to deal with this thing we call racism. We all are impacted and have been deceived. We all need healing and to walk out of darkness.

Uncovering the Lie

On the surface, the charge of reverse racism seems ridiculous in the context of the historic and current inequities between whites and BIPOC. Yet when we look deeper, we recognize that it's an expression of white privilege and energized by a range of negative emotions. This leads to an attitude that indicates: "Don't confuse me with the facts, I know what I believe." Only by raising questions that probe the sources of those beliefs and feelings underlying them can we begin to shake white people from their delusion. While we may be perceived as a threat, in fact we are helping many impacted by a racist system that keeps them from seeing social and economic inequities for what they are. This intention to help, rather than threaten, must guide our efforts to free them from the lie of reverse racism.

White Liberals

*It's the responsibility of those of us who come from
privilege ... to engage in the hard work of building
accountability to others and ourselves.*

—Jordan Flaherty

Turning the Focus on Ourselves

Up to this point, we have been discussing how we can talk with white
people about racial issues in a constructive and potentially transformative way. The white persons whom we have referenced have had minimal
interaction with BIPOC and engaged in limited critical thinking about
issues of race in the United States. They are not white nationalists speaking into an echo chamber of fear, hate and bigotry; rather, they generally
see themselves as good people trying to make a living, take care of their
families, spend time with friends, be concerned citizens and just live their
lives. Yet when the issue of race comes up, they feel flustered, guilty,
withdrawn and defensive, being made responsible for something they
did not do or create. They don't think of themselves as racist and may
claim to have colleagues or friends of color, but they are afraid and even
turned off by what they see as a rising tide of racial strife and challenge.

Those reading this book, I assume, see racism as a polarizing force in
U.S. society. They recognize that if our society is to hold together in the
coming decades, whites and BIPOC need to find a way to live together
equitably, fairly and empathetically. This book has been an exploration
of how we can bring more white people to a recognition that racism is a
vital issue for them, their children and society as a whole.

In this chapter I turn our attention to white liberals, those who have tak-
en the time to learn about the multifaceted and multidimensional nature
of racism in U.S. society. They may be actively involved in supporting

causes and organizations to change racist laws and racist institutional structures. They may have developed meaningful friendships with BI-POC. They consider themselves "woke" to the realities of racism and the need for change. I am one of these white people, and am guessing that many of those reading this book fall into this category as well.

The reality is that we "woke" white liberals are often blind to our own racism and the racist practices that create barriers between us and the people with whom we want to work toward an antiracist society. This chapter also addresses the manner in which we need to interrogate ourselves.

Characteristics of the White Liberal

Most white liberals become involved in the struggle for racial justice because of what Mark Warren calls "moral shock."[1] In his study of white racial-justice activists, Warren found that there were particularly heinous events that caused the white activists he interviewed to become involved in fighting racism. Often those experiences included things they had heard and learned in relationships with BIPOC. Warren found that many white activists defined themselves as "moral actors" seeking to build a more racially just and equitable society.[2]

Whether or not they become activists, I think a similar dynamic causes many whites to take on a more progressive view regarding race relations. They see the violence and injustice and can no longer ignore or turn away from it. Often this awareness naturally leads to the question: *What can I, as a white person, do to end racial injustice?* However, Sullivan[3] points out that the problem with this question is that it ignores the fact that other white people, white privileging institutions and socioeconomic policies that favor them have shaped them. Sullivan suggests that the first question whites must ask themselves is, "How have our behaviors, attitudes and values been shaped by white dominant culture?" As Robin DiAngelo expressed in an interview: "All of us have been shaped by the cultural water that we swim in. All white people have internalized a racist worldview. Let me own that. As a result of being raised as a white person in this society, I have a racist worldview."[4]

Thus white liberals must begin with themselves, recognizing that their intentions and goodwill often come from a place that is actually destructive to the very thing they are trying to accomplish. In relationship to other whites, white liberals have what University of Kansas professor Zak Foste[5] calls an "enlightenment narrative." They see themselves as more enlightened on race issues than other whites and view those others as uninformed or ignorant. They see it as their role to educate and set other whites straight on the nature of racism. At the same time, these enlightened ones fail to acknowledge their need for continued learning and exposure to the influence of racism on their lives. They feel they have arrived and need no further growth. When I talk with predominantly white groups about these issues, often the ones most offended are those who feel they are aware and enlightened on these topics. How dare I suggest they need continued growth and experience.

At the heart of the enlightenment narrative is a high level of certainty about one's antiracist position. Often that displays itself as a deep desire to be seen as a "good white person" who has transcended the impact of the racism and whiteness at the heart of the culture. However, these same whites fail to see how they perpetuate racist practices and structures in their efforts to do good. Antiracism efforts become acts of individual willpower and personal change, and don't deal with the wider systemic issues affecting everyone, both white and non-white.

This sense of enlightenment is often perceived by BIPOC as a "superiority complex."[6] The motivation of many white liberals to help BIPOC comes from pity and sympathy. They all too often act as if BIPOC are in need and that whites need to help them. It's what causes some well-meaning whites to teach in urban schools and work in social-service positions, and for white church groups to do "urban mission trips." White liberals too often see communities of color as full of needs crying out for their attention while they overlook the richness of local culture, ignore the wisdom of people's lived experiences and fail to appreciate the resourcefulness of their actions.

In multiple studies of whites in various settings, Dupree and Fiske[7] found that well-intentioned whites concerned about racial injustices often expressed and demonstrated warmth, kindness and caring toward BIPOC but did not respect their knowledge and competence. These whites felt it was their job to do what the BIPOC were unable to do for themselves, rather than join them in their ongoing efforts at change and improvement. As a result, they found it difficult to relationally connect with BIPOC, and those in their lives felt devalued, dismissed and insulted. Upon reading about this study, *Philadelphia Inquirer* columnist Solomon Jones noted that it brought to mind "the adage I've often heard from older Blacks. It goes something like this: I'd rather deal with white people from down South. At least with them you know where you stand."[8]

Before white liberals can make a significant difference, they must come to terms with what it means to be white, understanding how whiteness influences their thoughts, attitudes and actions. As African American philosopher Lucius Outlaw writes: "White people need to get off their duffs and begin figuring out what whiteness might mean other than the ongoing domination of BIPOC."[9] In other words, unless white liberals do this self-reflecting work with each other, they will continue to cause harm where they thought they were helping. They must come to terms their own liberal form of racism.

Liberal Racism

This is based on the assumption that having the right attitudes and saying the right things proves one's antiracist stance. White liberals point the finger at other whites who use racially derogatory language, wave Confederate flags, participate in white nationalist marches, and oppose laws and policies designed to achieve racial equity. They see themselves as the good whites because they joined in a Black Lives Matter march or wear a T-shirt with Dr. King's picture on it. Yet they balk at suggestions that their actions (or lack of action), micro-aggressions or daily choices betray a lack of sustained commitment to the institutional and systematic change that must occur for racial justice to be achieved.

Liberal racism places well-meaning whites in a caring and compassionate role, while regarding BIPOC as needy and subservient. Thus, while emphasizing the role of whites to address the injustices of racism, liberal racism maintains the racial hierarchy that makes whites dominant and BIPOC subordinate. Instead of calling whites to be allies and partners in the struggle against racism, liberal racism shows whites as saviors.

I count myself among those who would be called a white liberal, and more times than I wish to count I have been called out for my liberal racism. I have made comments to friends of color that betrayed my micro-aggressions and then gotten defensive when those were called to my attention. I have failed to support the efforts of colleagues of color to achieve greater equity and recognition for their workplace contributions. I have attempted (and often succeeded) in taking center stage in a conversation, when the more qualified and authoritative person was a BIPOC. I have sometimes sought to protect BIPOCs because I thought they were vulnerable when they were quite capable of speaking and acting for themselves. I have made the mistake of assuming that my experience in daily life was the same as that of BIPOC, ignoring or denying the dynamics of racism that grant me privilege and construct barriers for them. The list could go on and it does.

White Saviors

This disturbing expression of white liberal racism leads to the white-savior mentality in people who feel it's their duty—even calling—to take the lead in an effort to help the poor, disenfranchised and victims of injustice. Yet instead of following the lead of others closer to the pain, they want to work on their own terms. While their motivations may be honorable, white saviors want to lead and direct the process rather than work in solidarity and consultation with those most affected by the injustice being addressed.

Flaherty[10] describes the characteristics of saviors in the following manner: Usually they are people who were raised in privilege and taught to have the knowledge and skills to rescue others. At the same time, they fail to account for the systems that give them power while disempowering others. Thus they are not about changing or challenging the unjust structures, but seek to find solutions within the existing systems. They want to help others without asking what kind of help they might need, and go by terms such as "change agent," "activist" and "social entrepreneur" without having spent significant time with the people they are purporting to help. In the end, any change or improvement goes to increase their status and not to those they are seeking to help. Flaherty suggests that the savior mentality is a twisted form of racial privilege, a way of exercising one's position and power for good causes with little or no cost.

Flaherty writes that "the very origin story of the United States forms the core of the savior project."[11] The nonprofit sector, humanitarian causes, the voluntourism industry and Christian missions are expressions of this ethos. While they profess to be helping "the less fortunate," the real attraction is the emotional high and acclamation they receive upon completion of the trip or project. Whether they have built a house, dug a well or healed the sick, their good works have not done anything to address the root causes of the suffering they were sent to relieve. While such works are not without merit, one must be careful to see who really gains in the transaction. As Flaherty says: "Any aid not accountable to the community it seeks to serve and doesn't address fundamental systemic issues behind the problems it claims to address, will only reinforce an unjust system."[12]

When saviorism is directed toward communities of color, it often reinforces internalized racism among those being served. People begin to believe they don't have the power or agency to address the needs they have and therefore turn to the privileged person to rescue them. While in tragic short-term events like natural disasters there is a need for rescue, if the effort doesn't quickly move toward training and empowering the people in need to take over, the dependency increases and underlying problems are not addressed.

More disturbingly, the effect of the white-savior mentality serves to hide the leadership and hard work of those already in the community and instead gives credit to the white outsiders. I have been in several gatherings where BIPOC talk about "being invisible." Instead of getting credit for their efforts, the attention is given to the white people who happened to have recently showed up. These colleagues of color reminded those who are white that we should be wary and deflect that attention, and support and affirm the leaders who have been working diligently long before the white people showed up. In other words, whites can enter a situation without savior intentions, but still must be wary of being put in that position just by their presence.

To avoid the trap of the white-savior mentality, they must remain cognizant of their privilege and make themselves accountable to indigenous and local leaders. For example, a white woman, Berkeley Carnine, went to work with the Dine (commonly called Navajo) people in the southwest U.S. and realized this dilemma. Upon reflection, she identified certain guidelines for keeping perspective: Know whose turf you are on, ask permission to be involved, know where your resources come from and how they affect the people you are seeking to help, and be aware of the systemic racism involved in the situation in which you are supposedly helping.[13] More succinctly, as they seek to address trauma and suffering in communities, whites must also be committed to addressing the institutional and systemic forces that have caused such suffering.

Some might respond to these caveats as a message for white people not to get involved in addressing racial injustice. That is not my intention. First, we need to realize that we must work *with* those we seek to serve and not simply do things *to* and *for* them. More importantly, we need to follow community leadership and listen to those closest the problems. We may have insights and resources that can be helpful, but we need to let go of our need to control and do things our way, and instead trust that people know the answers to their problems better than outsiders. Whites may have access to resources and political connections that can be of help, but they must not act on their own, thereby consciously or unconsciously falling into the trap of white saviorism.

Decentering Whites and Whiteness
Caitlin Breedlove is a white antiracist activist who formerly worked at the Highland Research and Education Center in New Market, Tennessee, as well as for Southerners on New Ground (SONG), an LGBT justice organization. In an interview with Flaherty, she offered guidelines for would-be saviors. Activists who come from privilege need to think about how they are centering or decentering themselves in their work. Are they receiving feedback from people over whom they don't have power?[14] Jeff Hitchcock from the Center for the Study of White Culture adds that "the best way to combat the savior mentality is to act collectively for systemic change in a way that is accountable to communities affected."[15] At the

same time, white antiracists must not allow themselves to be cowered by challenges to their words and actions. They should take risks, and willing to be corrected and enlightened by those most directly affected, while open to difficult conversations and willing to listen.

Would-be white saviors also need to question their motives for being involved in antiracist work in the first place. Are they trying to fill a gap in their lives to be noticed and acclaimed for their concern for racial justice? Are they only doing the work to have something to put on a résumé or college application? Are they able to be involved for the long haul without the need to be in leadership or always get credit for gains made? Are they willing to follow the leadership of BIPOC and support them even when they may not always understand what's going on? Are they willing to grow, learn and open up as they work with others for justice?

Decentering oneself as a white savior involves as much unlearning as it does learning. As Flaherty points out, "For people born into privilege decentering yourself can feel difficult. It involves giving up a certain amount of privilege and when you are accustomed to privilege, equality feels like oppression."[16] While we focus on the violence and trauma foisted on others, we must also ask how our privilege may have in some way contributed to their hurt and suffering. These are difficult questions that don't lead to clear or easy answers and can stay throughout one's life. Well-meaning whites must let go of their need for credit, entitlement and privilege, while seeking to live and work in solidarity with those most affected by the systemic racism at the heart of U.S. culture.

Such a process requires deep reflection and even a spiritual transformation. In his book, *Pedagogy of the Oppressed*,[17] Paulo Freire challenges social-justice leaders to recognize that in varying degrees "the oppressor [is] housed within them,"[18] and that they need to undergo a profound internal change, a "conversion to the people."[19] This involves seeing oneself in solidarity with the people one seeks to help and not as somehow distinct from them. In much the same way, whites seeking to work for racial justice must go through that kind of conversion experience so as to be truly united with those they are seeking to help.[20]

Responding to the White Liberal

When talking with a white person who exhibits the characteristics of the white liberal or savior, one must be firm and even confrontive at times. Ironically, those most willing to point out the racism in others are often resistant to examining their own racism. Our first questions should seek to elicit their story. How and where did they grow up? What were the circumstances and events that led them to their current understanding of racism? In what ways did they receive privilege? What have been some significant efforts in which they have sought to fight racism in our society? What have they learned about the complexity of racism, and about themselves?

Then it's important to explore their understanding of racism. In their view, what makes one a racist or nonracist? How is this understanding of racism shaped by systemic and institutional structures? What is their understanding of privilege? How have they sought to address that privilege? Is it possible for white people to have good intentions while doing and saying things that are racist? Have they ever done that?

Some whites may see themselves as activists. If so, how are they making themselves accountable to BIPOC? Are they able to work under the leadership of others, particularly leaders of color? In what ways have they received accolades for their work and deprived those accolades from people in the community they are trying to help? How are they growing in their understanding of the pernicious effects of whiteness even as they try to undo it?

Such questions are not designed to discourage whites from caring and being involved in antiracist work, but to keep them honest. Often their intentions may be honorable, but their words and actions can cause BIPOC around them to feel devalued. Through no conscious fault of their own, the system and culture may highlight them, while overlooking the BIPOC at their side. The white liberal and white savior must come to see that such questions are not about diminishing their work, but rather empowering those most disempowered by the ravages of racism in our culture.

In essence, the white liberal and savior must come to realize that unlearning and challenging racism within oneself is a lifelong endeavor.

Even while working and advocating for change, they must realize that their activism doesn't exempt them from ongoing self-reflection. White people can be allies for the cause of racial justice, but they must count the cost, which is both political and personal, and is always unfolding.

Interrupting Overt Racism

*If you don't speak up, you're surrendering part
of yourself. You're letting bigotry win.*

—Bob Carolla

Taking the Risk

The impetus for writing this book was to provide assistance to whites and
BIPOC in talking with their white friends, co-workers and family members about racism. However, there are times when people in our relational circles express such racist vitriol and take such hateful actions that
seeking to engage them in conversation is neither possible nor desirable.
At such times, one must speak up and take a stand against overt racist
talk and action. Choosing to remain silent sends the message that such
inexcusable actions are acceptable, thus reinforcing the white solidarity
that must be disrupted.

One time in a workshop I asked a group of white people to share experiences where they had witnessed racism. One man (I will call John) told
a story about attending a high-school basketball game. On the visiting
team was a Black player, the only one on the court. A white man a few
rows behind John began shouting "Get that n----r!" He repeatedly taunt-
ed the young man on the court. No one in the stands confronted the man
until John stood up, turned around and said to the taunter, "Enough!
We don't talk like that here." John turned back around and sat down,
and the man behind him was silent for the rest of the game. However, as
the game ended and John started to leave, he heard a voice behind say
"n----r lover!"

This story wouldn't be so sad if it were not so common. The fact that so
often overt racists are otherwise well-functioning individuals makes it all
the more troubling. One would like to chalk it up to ignorance or lack

of emotional development. Moreover, the fact that only one person in the stands was willing to call out the overt racism is equally disturbing. People making such statements, like that man in the stands, are in our schools, workplaces and sometimes even in our families; it is all too easy to simply say nothing.

To stand up as John did is to take a great risk. First, others may remain mute; one can feel very alone. Second, there is the risk of being labeled and excluded by other whites. John was called a n----r lover. Third, sometimes there is even the fear of physical danger. As a 6'2" healthy male, I am not easily intimidated, but there have been a few times I feared that confronting one's racism could get physical. Yet if committed to challenging racism, these are risks that must be taken.

Responding to Everyday Bigotry

The Southern Poverty Law Center collected hundreds of stories of "Everyday Bigotry" from people across the country, which are told in a publication called *Speak Up: Responding to Everyday Bigotry*. In this book, people have shared anecdotes of encountering those making racist, sexist and homophobic statements, and how they responded, involving situations people faced in their families, at work, with neighbors and in schools. The editors then developed "Six Steps to Speaking Up Against Everyday Bigotry." [1]

The first is to be ready. Racism in our society should not surprise us, so we should be prepared to respond. Communications professor Marsha Houston writes: "Summon your courage, whatever it takes to get that courage, that source of courage is for you."[2] To help with courage, people should think ahead about what they would say if a racist statement is made, perhaps starting with an innocent question like, "What made you say that?" Or "What do you mean by saying that?" Or like John: "Enough. We don't talk like that here."

Tim Wise, the noted antiracist speaker, suggests that using humor can sometimes work in such situations. One time he was the invited speaker at a college event; afterward, he went out with some students for dinner and they were joined by a fellow student who had not attended the lecture. The newcomer told a racist joke involving Black people and the group got uncomfortably silent. Wise spoke up: "You know, my mother is Black." The joke-teller immediately got embarrassed and started apologizing. Wise then said "Just kidding!" He proceeded to ask why the joke was okay as long as no one had a Black mother.[3] He used a joke to confront the racist comment and open up the possibility for conversation.

Whether having a semi-prepared response, question or playful trick, the point is to call attention to the comment or action. Being prepared doesn't allow the racist joke to linger or go unchallenged.

Second, one should identify the offensive behavior. This can be tricky. The key is to note the actions or statements without labeling the person. One wants to delegitimize the words spoken, but not the person speaking them. If a person calls another a bigot or racist, a barrier will go up and the conversation will end. For example, in response to a pejorative description of undocumented immigrants, one might say: "So you are saying that all these people who traveled hundreds of miles to come to this country and who work two and three jobs are lazy? Is that what you are saying?" The point is to name the racist comment and challenge it.

Third, one should appeal to the person's values and principles. If they're familiar, one can appeal to their friendship and the respect they have for one another. If it's a family member, to their common family values. Sometimes overt racism is a regular part of one's family life and so appealing to the family's values might not be desirable. In that case, one should appeal to values such as love, civility and respect for others' human dignity. As people opposed to racism, we should know why we believe as we do and not be hesitant to let the values behind our views known.

Fourth, a person needs to set limits on what to put up with while staying connected.[4] No one can change another person; people can only change themselves. So one must make clear what to allow. One might say, "Don't tell racist jokes when you're around me" or "If you are going to carry on like that, just count me out." The key is to stay connected while drawing the line on what to tolerate. It would be easy to walk away and not interact with the person. However, our relationship with that person and the willingness to stay connected, even when we dislike what a person does or says, carries more influence than we realize.

In Family Systems Theory, this practice of drawing boundaries while staying connected is called self-differentiation. Renowned family-systems therapists Michael Kerr and Murray Bowen define self-differentiation as "the ability to be in emotional contact with others yet still autonomous in one's emotional functioning" with them.[5] In other words, a self-differentiated person is able to stay emotionally connected to another person without being emotionally dependent for a sense of self-worth. The ability to remain firm in one's convictions while staying emotionally connected to another is a powerful influence on thinking and action.[6] This is why it's so important to continually reflect and work on one's prejudices and biases, even when seeking to confront others with their biases. To remain connected, we don't have to excuse or ignore one's racist behavior, and to do that we must differentiate ourselves while staying in that relationship.

Fifth is to find allies or be an ally to others. The work of resisting and overcoming racism is not for superheroes who go out on their own. One needs to seek out similarly minded colleagues and friends with whom to share and reflect. People need folks who can listen, empathize and encourage as together they confront the racism around them, as well as friends who will lovingly correct and call them out when they stumble into old patterns of thought and action.

Finally, the person seeking to confront overt racism must be vigilant. Opportunities to speak about our experiences and perspectives will present themselves if we are looking for them. "Change happens slowly. People make small steps, typically not large ones. Stay prepared and keep speaking up. Don't risk silence."[7] The failure to speak up when the situation presents itself diminishes us and the other person.

An Example to Follow

Qasim Rashid is a Muslim who lives in Virginia and was a Democratic candidate running for a seat in the U.S. Congress. One week, Rashid received several "deeply hurtful anti-Muslims tweets," all from a man named Oscar Dillon, whose wife suffers from a life-threatening disease. Both of them are retired and live on a fixed income. The treatments for her illness are expensive, such that by the 23rd of every month they are out of money.

Rashid decided to try finding out who his disgruntled, anti-Muslim critic was. He found Dillon online and discovered that he had set up a GoFundMe page to help allay the cost of his wife's treatments. Rashid then donated to the fund and encouraged others to do so as well. Dillon, seeing what had happened, responded to Rashid with an apology and the two were eventually able to meet in person. Dillon shared that the 9/11 attacks had generated in him a hatred of "radical Islam" and by extension all Muslims. Rashid's courage, generosity and kindness broke though Dillon's hardness, hate and blindness.[8]

What is so impressive about this story is not only Qasim Rashid's courage to reach out to an overtly racist critic, but also his ability to see past the hate to the underlying pain. Oscar Dillon's racist comments masked deep personal suffering. Tweeting anti-Muslim rants at Rashid was an easy way to vent. For centuries, people have scapegoated others for the deep hurt in their lives. Belittling a person of another race, ethnicity, citizenship status or religion has been a sordid side of our nation's history. Often degrading others is easier than facing one's own powerlessness.

While it's not always the case, all too often the racist bigotry spewed on the Internet, chanted at white nationalist rallies, dog-whistled at alt-right meetings, echoed in school halls and vented by members of Congress are cries of pain. The fact that these acts and statements arise from personal pain doesn't excuse them, but allows us to remember that behind the overt racism is a person who is living below his basic human dignity. In confronting them with respect, we offer them the opportunity to redeem their personhood. Quasim Rashid's example is one all would do well to follow.

Relentless Responsibility

Few are guilty, but all are responsible.
—Abraham Joshua Heschel

Disrupting Whiteness: A Strategy

In this book, I have attempted to lay out a strategy for disrupting whiteness, of breaking through white silence and avoiding the reality of racism in the laws, policies, structures and culture of U.S. society. Given the political tribalism and racial polarization of society, this is not an easy task. The death of George Floyd, Breonna Taylor and others, and the marches and demonstrations that followed, have brought issues of institutional and systemic racism to the fore. While many white people have joined in the calls for substantive change, many other whites are being challenged to come to terms with the reality of racism, with whiteness, at all levels of U.S. society. Many whites are scared at what changes might come and political leaders like Donald Trump have sought to stoke those fears for their own political advantage. And yet the changes being called for in this book, as well as the ongoing demonstrations, will not just benefit BIPOC, but also the well-being of whites.

In *Tears We Cannot Stop: A Sermon to White America*, African American scholar Michael Eric Dyson writes: "You don't get whiteness from your genes. It's a social inheritance that is passed on to you as a member of a particular group. And it's killing us and quiet as it's kept, it's killing you too."[1] *It's killing you too.* Dyson goes onto say, speaking to white people: "The only way to save our nation and yes save yourselves, is to let go of whiteness and the vision of American history it supports."[2] In much the same way, James Baldwin describes how the white people he encountered always wanted to deny or dismiss the racist history of America, while at the same time being crippled by that history. He notes that "they suffer enormously from the resulting personal incoherence."[3] The logic of white racism is a virus infecting all within its reach.

But there's more according to Jennifer Harvey; in this incoherent state, whites are trapped "in a state of profound moral crisis."[4] As much as whites may profess to be morally good and ethically right in their daily lives, the privilege and power afforded them by the power of whiteness renders them morally and ethically degenerate. It's not that whites are somehow inherently immoral. Rather it's that whites have allowed white supremacy to define their identities, shape their institutions and infect their laws. The issue for whites is one of integrity; will we live up to our creed that all men and women, regardless of race, culture, religion or background are created equal and should be treated as such? For the good of the BIPOC who suffer discrimination in its myriad forms, as well as for whites whose person is on the line, whiteness must be disrupted and rendered powerless.

Few Are Guilty—All Are Responsible

On January 14, 1963, Conservative Jewish rabbi Abraham Joshua Heschel rose to deliver the opening address at a conference on religion and race sponsored by the National Conference of Christians and Jews. In words biting with truth and urgency, Heschel named racism as "satanism, unmitigated evil" and "a cancer of the soul." He called upon white Americans, and particularly white religious leaders, to speak and act prophetically against racist acts and practices in their lives, their faith communities and society in general. He called them to be less concerned about the "purity of their dogma" and more about "the integrity of their love." He described the issue not just as a matter of individual bias, but also as the result of a corrupted moral state of U.S. society. In conclusion he announced, "Few are guilty, but all are responsible."[5]

That phrase—"Few are guilty, but all are responsible"—has become a refrain against all forms of oppression that we need to take up today. If white people today are guilty of anything, it's not for what has happened in the past, for what their ancestors did or did not do. Rather, it's their inaction and indifference to change what they know to be true. It's acting as if the myths and lies of history have had no impact on the present. It's regarding as trivial and meaningless the hundreds of thousands of school children who don't receive a basic quality education, the BIPOC who have been targeted for incarceration and violence, the white nationalists who shout "Blood and Soil" invoking a Nazi spirit, and the politicians who use racial bigotry as a tool to get elected. White guilt lies in seeing and hearing such things and doing nothing, acting as if they are of no concern or consequence.

The work of addressing racism in predominantly white communities, churches, workplaces and social settings is the work in which white people of conscience must be engaged. Few are guilty, but all are responsible. As long as the vast majority of white people continue to deny, diminish or run away from the racism in their souls and in the laws, policies and structures of society, all will continue to suffer. For the sake of all—BIPOC and white people—we cannot allow that to happen.

Bringing racism into the conversation with white people often triggers their fragility. I have stressed that this is a conversation many whites need but don't want to have. These talks take courage and commitment; to work for racial understanding and justice cannot be rooted in social acceptance, material success or personal gain, but rather in the foundational promises to all citizens to enjoy "life, liberty and the pursuit of happiness." Our commitment must be grounded in the fundamental assertions of our faith traditions and moral codes. Racism in its many forms is an unmitigated evil, a cancer, a scourge on the face of our society, and must not be allowed to operate without strong and persistent opposition and resistance.

We must be unrelenting and persistent in our efforts to address racism in its personal, relational and systemic forms. Quoting abolitionist William Lloyd Garrison, Heschel said: "I will be harsh as truth and uncompromising as justice."[6] In our own day, the hallowed principles of truth and justice are too often compromised. From the White House to Congress, from the office building to the neighborhood, truth and justice are up for grabs and compromise. For this reason we must act with persistence and moral audacity.

Be Relentless

In conversations with our friends, co-workers and loved ones, we may find ourselves coming to what feels like an impasse. People will say they just don't want to talk about this "race thing" anymore. But if racism is evil and a cancer, failing to disrupt whiteness allows our white friends, family members and co-workers to remain morally sick and spiritually bankrupt. Few may be guilty, but all are responsible and so we who seek to address the racism at the heart of this society, particularly in the white community, must be relentless.

In this book, I have drawn from my experiences and study of the dynamics of racism about how to talk to white people about race and racism in our society. I have provided insights into the defenses and rationalizations white people often use to deflect conversations about race and ways to address those defenses. I have emphasized the importance of ongoing conversations in personal relationships, inviting people to tell their stories and drawing them into dialogue using probing questions. This can be slow, painful, long-range work. Yet our friends and colleagues of color call us to take this up in concert with efforts to change laws, policies and institutions that denigrate and discriminate against them. I have also stressed that while we are talking with others, we must continue to work on our own internalized racism.

There may have been a time when white people in remote areas of the United States might have been able to honestly say they did not know that things were so destructive and discriminatory. However, with 24-hour news cycles and social media, such a claim cannot be made today. Many whites can honestly say that they are struggling economically and feel like they are in a contest with BIPOC in some sort of race to the bottom. However, few if any whites can relate to cases of unarmed BIPOC being harmed, arrested or killed for asserting their basic rights like Eric Garner, Trayvon Martin, Philando Castile, Sandra Bland, Tamir Rice, Breonna Taylor, George Floyd, Jacob Blake and countless others. Few whites can honestly justify the disproportionate discrimination against BIPOC when it comes to school funding, healthcare, criminal justice, housing and employment opportunities. White people may not understand why these discrepancies exist, but the discrepancies themselves are undisputed public knowledge. So the issue is not one of having access to the truth of racism, but whether one is willing to see, hear and acknowledge that truth.

Poet Maya Angelou put it this way:

> Take the blinders from your vision,
> take the padding from your ears,
> and confess you've heard me crying,
> and admit you've seen my tears.[7]

While white people today may not have created the laws and structures that ensure inequality and discrimination, we know they are there and all are now responsible to address them. Few are guilty, but all are responsible. It starts with us.

Epilogue

If you don't know the kind of person I am
And you don't know the kind the person you are
a pattern that others may prevail in the world
and following the wrong god home we may miss our star.
—William Stafford, *A Ritual to Read to Each Other*

As this book goes to print, Joe Biden has been elected the 46th president of the United States and Kamala Harris becomes the first woman and person of color to be elected as vice-president. Their campaign to victory was not easy and the months before they took office were in some ways as chaotic and conflict-ridden as the path leading to their victory. Donald Trump waged a campaign of distraction, seeking to suppress people's ability vote and the right for their vote to be counted. His rallies were often characterized by rousing invectives and bold lies designed to generate fear and anger in his followers. He regularly used racist dog-whistle tropes[1] and welcomed the support white nationalist militias. He even claimed that the only way he could lose the election was if the Democrats conducted some sort of mass campaign of voter fraud, and used numerous means to discount and undermine mail-in balloting. Those who believed and voted for him can only be left with a level of distrust in the election process and those elected to lead our country.

As the political campaigns carried on, the number of deaths due to COVID-19 continued to climb to the highest levels since the pandemic began. While the rates of infections and deaths were disproportionately weighted toward those who were older, poor and/or BIPOC, no race or ethnic group and no age group were exempt. In fact, many reports stressed that one of the fastest rates of infection was in the 25- to 44-year-old range.[2] Even though vaccines to protect people from the virus are now becoming available, widespread vaccination will not be available until at least the spring of 2021. Because of President Trump's dismissal of the virus' danger, many individuals have chosen to avoid taking even the most elemental precautions like wearing masks, maintaining proper physical distancing and participating in large-group events (like many of Trump rallies). While Biden is a strong advocate of these basic actions, he has received significant pushback from those who believed and followed Trump's lead.

As a result of the pandemic, many people have lost their jobs or had their work hours severely cut, such that poverty and unemployment rates have risen to levels not seen in decades. Many businesses, particularly in the restaurant sector, have been forced to close or are just making it. A polarized Congress has been unable to agree on and pass further financial relief, and Republican efforts to abolish the Affordable Care Act have been put before the Supreme Court at a time when the health of countless people is being threatened like never before.

Among all of these issues are the continued calls for significant change from the Movement for Black Lives and related organizations, which have spawned a general uprising among BIPOC and their white allies in areas such as policing, incarceration, healthcare, education and housing. This movement for change has been accompanied by an increasingly resistant belligerence from white nationalist groups, some of whom are armed militias. The attempted kidnapping of Michigan Governor Gretchen Whitmer shows the extent to which these domestic terrorists will go to have their way.

Joe Biden repeatedly contended that he decided to run for president to "heal the soul of the nation." Donald Trump's divisive campaign and the continuing disruptive efforts of some of his Republican colleagues make Biden's efforts to bring healing all that much more difficult. While I don't doubt the sincerity of Biden's intentions, healing will not come at the level of politics. In fact, I fear that the political and corporate realms of our society may be the last to change. The change we seek is a grassroots change, a change in relationships and of culture.

Noted social-change theorist John Kania indicates that before there can be change at the level of laws and policies, there must be a change in the culture that informs and undergirds structural and policy decisions.

According to Kania, one of the most significant areas where cultural change begins is in the realm of relationships. People need to move out of their social and political echo chambers and begin conversations with people whose worldviews and hopes for the country are widely different. And these conversations can't be shouting matches where we simply talk past each other; there must be authentic listening and engagement.[3]

This is where *Disrupting Whiteness* seeks to provide a road map to healing. I have provided some principles of engagement: storytelling, active listening and dialogue. The goal is to first learn the stories that lie behind the beliefs and values people espouse, and to follow up with questions informed by an understanding of the dynamics of racism and white supremacy that I have discussed. My call to readers is to engage in dialogue with persons who deny or resist the reality of racism in our society, to find common ground and open a space to share perspectives and stories. The process is neither formulaic nor quick and easy. Culture change, like developing relationships, takes time and a commitment to hang in there with the other person.

This past summer I put a Black Lives Matter sign on my front lawn. A couple of days later, a neighbor whose back porch looks toward my back patio put up a Thin Blue Line flag[4] over his back railing, a symbol of police solidarity and more recently a response that "blue lives matter." In some quarters, this flag has also been associated with white supremacy. That flag was a response to my sign. I need to introduce myself (we have never actually met) and ask if we can have a conversation about how we came to the views we have. I need to understand why my Black Lives Matter sign was offensive to him and if in fact his flag was his response. I need to hear the stories behind his actions, and hopefully he will be open not only to share, but to listen to my point of view.

Kania says that sometimes the barriers to change lie within our worldviews, attitudes and actions or inactions.[5] If I am not willing to take the risk of engaging with folks like my neighbor, whose attitudes and views are ones with which I strongly disagree, then healing will never come to my neighbor, my community and my country. *Disrupting Whiteness* challenges us to reach across the caverns that separate us as a nation.

If there is going to be healing in this nation, it has to begin on the individual and relational level. Groups working for changes in laws, policies and practices must continue to be supported, but those structural changes will not take root and last if they are not accompanied by cultural changes, which in part will come by transformative relationships that help white people realize they have much to gain with racial justice and equity. They will be safer, healthier and freer from the guilt, anger, defensiveness and denial that historic white body trauma has inflicted upon them. In so doing, we can move from a nation of us versus them to a nation truly living out the promise to be *We the People* whom our nation's founders intended us to be.

Endnotes

Preface

1. Centers for Disease Control and Prevention (CDC). "History of the 1918 Flu Pandemic." https://www.cdc.gov/flu/pandemic-resources/1918-commemoration/1918-pandemic-history.htm

2. Naomi Thomas. "Study Finds Racial and Ethnic Disparities in Covid-19 hospitalizations," *CNN*, August 17, 2020. https://www.cnn.com/2020/08/17/health/covid-19-hospitalizations-racial-ethnic-disparities-study/index.html

3. Li Zhou. "Trump's Racist References to the Coronavirus Are His Latest Effort to Stoke Xenophobia," *Vox*, June 23, 2020. https://www.vox.com/2020/6/23/21300332/trump-coronavirus-racism-asian-americans

4. Erin Donaghue. "2,120 Hate Incidents Against Asian Americans Reported During Coronavirus Pandemic," *CBS News*, July 2, 2020. https://www.cbsnews.com/news/anti-asian-american-hate-incidents-up-racism/

5. Bill McCarthy. "The Death of George Floyd: What You Need to Know," *Politifact*, May 29, 2020. Politifact.com/article/2020/may/29/death-george-floyd-what-you-need-know/

6. The impact of Black Lives Matter is also discussed in Ch. 3 "Whiteness and White Supremacy."

7. Debra Thompson. "An Exoneration of Black Rage," *The South Atlantic Quarterly*, 116 no. 3 (2017): 457-481.

8. Quoted in Thompson, op. cit., p. 460.

9. In 2016 the head of Minneapolis Police Officers Federation referred to Black Lives Matter as a terrorist organization (https://www.officer.com/command-hq/news/12215638/minneapolis-police-union-head-calls-black-lives-matter-terrorist-group). Rudy Giuliani, president Trump's lawyer has referred to Black Lives Matter as a "domestic terror group" (https://thehill.com/homenews/media/510953-giuliani-says-black-lives-matter-is-domestic-terrorist-group). President Trump has called them "a symbol of hate." (https://www.cnn.com/2020/07/01/politics/donald-trump-black-lives-matter-confederate-race/index.html)

10. Bill Hutchinson. "Deaths at Protests from Kenosha to Portland, but Motive Tells Different Story," *ABC News*, September 8, 2020. https://abcnews.go.com/US/deaths-connected-protests-story-complicated/story?id=72724790

11. Layla F. Saad. *Me and White Supremacy: Combat Racism, Change the World and Become a Good Ancestor*. (Naperville, IL: Source Books, 2020).

12. Mike Laws. "Why We Capitalize 'Black' (and Not "White')," *Columbia Journalism Review*, June 16, 2020. https://www.cjr.org/analysis/capital-b-black-styleguide.php

Introduction

1. The Antifa (short for anti-fascist) movement is a loosely connected network of anarchists and far left militants who see the re-emergence of white nationalism and the presidency of President Donald Trump as move toward the U.S. moving toward fascism that was most clearly embodied in Benito Mussolini, the president of Italy during World War II. While having a range of left-leaning political perspectives, they share a common commitment to direct action, including resorting to various levels of violence. In rallies like that in Charlottesville they are often characterized by the wearing of black ski masks and a willingness to directly engage those with whom they disagree. See The Anti-Defamation League (n.d.). Who are Antifa. https://www.adl.org/ resources/ backgrounders/who-are-antifa

2. Joe Heim. "Recounting a Day of Rage, Violence and Death," *Washington Post*, August 14, 2017. https://www.washingtonpost.com/graphics/2017/local/charlottesville -timeline/

3. I should note that the very fact that I could go on vacation and NOT concern myself or be aware of such an overtly racist event, is an example of the immense privilege I have as a white person to NOT concern myself with this event. If I was a BIPOC or Jewish, this would have much have been an event much more difficult to ignore, as it would have been "my people" under attack literally and figuratively.

4. Tim Wise. *White Like Me: Reflections on Race from a Privileged Son.* (New York: Soft Skull Press, 2011); *Dear White America: Letter to a New Minority.* (San: Francisco: City Lights Books, 2012).

5. Robin DiAngelo. *What Does it Mean to be White: Developing White Racial Literacy.* (New York: Peter Lang, 2016); *White Fragility: Why It's So Hard for White People to Talk about Racism.* (Boston: Beacon Press, 2018).

6. Paul Kivel. *Uprooting Racism: How White People Can Work for Racial Justice.* (Gabriola Island, BC Canada: New Society Publishers, 2017).

7. Jeff Hitchcock. *Lifting the White Veil: An Exploration of White American Culture in a Multiracial Context.* (Roselle, NJ: Crandie, Dostie & Douglass Books Inc, 2002).

8. DiAngelo, *White Fragility.*

9. DiAngelo, *White Fragility*, 53.

10. DiAngelo, *White Fragility*, 57.

11. Robin DiAngelo presentation during the "White Fragility American Tour" (with Jack Hill), Philadelphia, PA, April 17, 2019.

12. More detail about this approach and the history of NewCORE discussed in Chapter 6.

13. Drick Boyd. *White Allies in the Struggle for Racial Justice.* (Maryknoll, NY: Orbis Books, 2015): 9.

14. The term "white allies" has come under criticism for being to passive, and so terms like "accomplices" and "co-conspirators" have been suggested. I have chosen to use the term

"allies" with the understanding that it requires active involvement and support for racial justice efforts and is not mere lip service.

15. These terms and others are addressed more fully in Chapters 2 and 3.

16. Scott Peck. *The Road Less Travelled: A New Psychology of Love, Traditional Values and Spiritual Growth.* (New York: Simon and Schuster, 1978).

Chapter 1: What Is Your Race Story?

1. I am indebted to Lisa Sharon Harper for this question. Lisa Sharon Harper. "The Little White Lie That Has Divided Our Country, " interview by Alex Gee. *Black Like Me*, Episode 21. http://blacklikeme.libsyn.com/lisa-sharon-harper-the-little-white-lie-that-has-divided-our-country; To understand the assimilation process, see Noel Ignatiev. *How the Irish Became White*. (New York Routledge, 1995).

Chapter 2: What Do We Mean by Race and Racism?

1. Associated Press. "House Rebukes GOP's Steve King Over Racist Remarks," *New York Times*, January 15, 2019. https://apnews.com/712ea1e8c9f24f8ba3afd7b680288a87 l; Trip Gabriel. "A Timeline of Steve King's Racist Remarks and Divisive Actions," *New York Times*, January 15, 2019. https://www.nytimes. com/2019/01/15/us/politics/ steve-king-offensive-quotes.html

2. Michael Omi and Harvey Winant. *Racial Formation in the United States, Third Edition*. (New York: Routledge, 2015).

3. Omi and Winant, *Racial Formation*, 3.

4. Indians as "savages."

5. 3/5 rule and non-voting of Indians.

6. David Unander. *Shattering the Myth of Race: Genetic Realities and Biblical Truths.* (Valley Forge: Judson Press, 2000): 8.

7. Takaki, *A Different Mirror*, 106.

8. Omi and Winant, *Racial Formation*, 110.

9. Omi and Winant, *Racial Formation*, 11.

10. DiAngelo, *White Fragility*, 19.

11. DiAngelo, *White Fragility*, 19.

12. This acting without awareness of power is what is referred to as white privilege and will be addressed in Chapter 3.

13. Iris de Leon-Hartshorn, Tobin Miller Shearer and Regina Shands-Stoltzfus. *Set Free: A Journey Toward Solidarity Against Racism.* (Scottdale, PA: Herald Press, 2001).

14. De Leon-Hartshorn et. al, *Set Free.*

15. Ibram X. Kendi. *How to Be an Antiracist.* (New York: One World Press, 2019).

16. Maria Kyrsan and Sarah Moberg. "A Portrait of African American and White Racial Attitudes," *University of Illinois Institute of Government & Public Affairs*, (September 9,

2016): 1. https://igpa.uillinois.edu/report/portrait-african-american-and-white-racial
-attitudes

17. Kyrsan & Moberg "Portrait;" Anna Marie Berry-Jester. "Attitudes Toward Racism and Inequality are Shifting. *ABC New*s, January 23, 2015. https://fivethirtyeight.com/ features/attitudes-toward-racism-and-inequality-are-shifting/

18. Tyrone Forman and Amanda E. Lewis. "Beyond Prejudice? Young Whites' Racial Attitudes in Post-Civil Rights America, 1976-2000." *American Behavioral Scientist*, 59 no. 11 (2015): 1394-1428.

19. Forman & Lewis," Beyond Prejudice?"

20. Southern Poverty Law Center. "White Nationalist" (no date). https://www.splcenter.org /fighting-hate/extremist-files/ideology/white-nationalist

21. Megan Padgett. "The Rise of the New White Nationalism in America," *University of Washington Digital Commons*, March 10, 2019. https://digitalcommons .tacoma.uw .edu/history_thesis/37; James Walsh. "Inside the White Nationalist Terrorist Movement in America, *New York Magazine*, December 19, 2019. https://nymag.com / intelligencer/2019/12/white-supremacy-terrorism-in-america-2019.html; Craig Franson and Charles Gallagher. "Why All the Hate? White Supremacy, White Nationalism and White Power," *La Salle University Digital Commons*, September 4, 2019. https:// digitalcommons.lasalee.edu/ explorercafe/84

22. Leslie Picca and Joe Feagin. *Two-Faced Racism: Whites in the Backstage and Frontstage.* (New York: Taylor and Francis, 2007).

23. Samuel Gaertner and John Dovidio. "The Aversive Form of Racism,'" in *Prejudice, Discrimination and Racism,* edited by John Dovidio and Samuel Gaertner. (Cambridge, MA: Academic Press, Inc., 1986), 61-89.

24. Derald Wing Sue. "Microaggressions: More Than Just Race," *Psychology Today*, November 17, 2010. https://www.psychologytoday.com/us/blog/microaggressions-in -everyday-life/201011/microaggressions-more-just-race

25. Richard Delgado and Jean Stefanic. *Critical Race Theory: An Introduction.* (New York: NYU Press, 2012):. 2.

26. I share an incident of being confronted on my microaggressions in an article. See Drick Boyd. "Autoethnography as a Tool for Transformative Learning About White Privilege," *Journal of Transformative Education*, 6 no. 3 (2008): 212-225.

27. Derald Wing Sue. *Microaggressions in Everyday Life: Race, Gender and Sexual orientation.* (Hoboken, NJ: John Wiley & Sons, 2010): 25-31.

28. Sue, *Microaggressions.*

29. Derald Wing Sue et. al (2007). "Racial Microaggressions in Everyday Life: Implications for Clinical Practice," *American Psychologist*, 62 no. 4 (2007): 271-286.

30. Sue et al, "Racial Microaggressions" has an extensive list of microaggressions organized various themes, 276-277.

31. For a fuller discussion of how racism gets institutionalized see Daria Roithmayr. *Reproducing Racism: How Everyday Choices Lock in White Advantage.* (New York: New York University Press, 2014).

32. Stephen Labaton. "Denny's Restaurants to Pay $54 Million in Race Bias Suits," *New York Times*, May 25, 1994. https://www.nytimes.com/1994/05/25/us/denny-s-restaurants-to-pay-54-million-in-race-bias-suits.html

33. Jonathan Stempel. "PepsiCo Settles U.S. Charge of Racial Bias in Hiring," *Reuters*, January 11, 2012. https://www.reuters.com/article/us-pepsico-bias-settlement/pepsico-settles-u-s-charge-of-racial-bias-in-hiring-idUSTRE80A2A720120111

34. Michelle Alexander. *The New Jim Crow: Mass Incarceration in the Age of Colorblindness.* (New York: The New Press, 2009).

35. Roithmayr, *Reproducing Racism.*

36. Gillian White. "The Data are Damning: How Race Influences School Funding," *The Atlantic*, September 30, 2015. http://www.theatlantic.com/business/archive/2015/09/publicschoolfundingandtheroleofrace/408085/

37. Ian Haney Lopez. *Dog Whistle Politics: How Coded Racial Appeals Have Reinvented Racism and Wrecked the Middle Class.* (New York :Oxford University Press, 2014).

38. Rotithmayr. *Reproducing Racism.*

39. Kendi. *Antiracist,* 9.

40. Kendi describes his experience with Stage 4 colon cancer. He realized to survive, he needed to make the difficult steps to undergo treatment. He says in the same way to overcome racism, we must do the hard work or our country will die because of racism. See Kendi, *Antiracist*, 233-237.

41. For more on the history of racism see Chapter 5.

Chapter 3: Whiteness and White Supremacy

1. Cited in Samuel Tanner. "Whiteness Is a White Problem," *English Education*, 51 no. 2 (2019): 182.

2. Tanner, "Whiteness."

3. Tanner, "Whiteness," 184.

4. Gloria Jean Watson, better known by her pen name bell hooks, is an American author, professor, feminist and social activist. The name "bell hooks" is purposely lower case and is borrowed from her maternal great-grandmother, Bell Blair Hooks https://en.wikipedia.org/wiki/Bell_hooks

5. bell hooks. *Yearning: Race, Gender and Cultural Politics.* (Cambridge, MA: South End Press, 1990): 54.

6. bell hooks. "Representations of Whiteness in the Black Imagination," in *White Privilege: Essential Readings on the Other Side of Racism, Fifth Edition*, edited by Paul Rothenberg. (New York: MacMillan 2016): 29.

7. W.E.B. Du Bois. "The Souls of White Folks," in *Darkwater: Voices From Within the Veil.* (Mineola, NY: Dover Publications,1990): 17-29.

8. Only later when I volunteered at a Black church in North Minneapolis did I come to realize that the same oppressive conditions afflicting Black folks in the South were also afflicting Black folks in my city. Moreover, the tragic murder of George Floyd at the hands of

Minneapolis policeman Derek Chauvin, uncovered a long history of harassment of BIPOC by the Minneapolis police.

9. Emily Bazelon. "White People are Noticing Something New: Their Own Whiteness," *New York Times*, June 13, 2018. https://www.nytimes.com/2018/06/13/magazine/white-people-are-noticing-something-new-their-own-whiteness.html

10. Ruth Frankenberg. "White Women, Race Ratters: The Social Construction of Whiteness," in *Critical Whiteness Studies: Looking Behind the Mirror*, edited by Richard Delgado and Jean Stefancic. (Philadelphia: Temple University Press, 1997): 632.

11. Delgado and Stefancic. *Critical Race Theory,* 84.

12. As discussed in Chapter 1, many European immigrants were at first considered as non-white, but through the process assimilation they eventually were granted to be white by the dominant culture.

13. Ruth Frankenberg. *White Women, Race Matters: The Social Construction of Whiteness.* (Minneapolis, MN: University of Minnesota Press, 1993): 1.

14. Cheryl Harris. "Whiteness As Property," *Harvard Law Review*, 166 no. 8 (1993): 1710-1791.

15. Ben Shapiro. "The Myth of White Privilege." Speech delivered at the University of Missouri, 2015. https://www.youtube.com/watch?v=VO6nOocD1yg

16. DiAngelo, *White Fragility*, 24.

17. Stephanie M. Wildman. "The Persistence of White Privilege," *Washington University Journal of Law & Policy*, 18 (2005): 245-265. https://openscholarship.wustl.edu/cgi /viewcontent.cgi?article=1262&context=law_journal_law_policy https://openscholarship.wustl.edu/law_journal_law_policy/vol18/iss1/11

18. Martin Luther King. "Letter From a Birmingham Jail," *Why We Can't Wait*. (New York Penguin Putnam Publishers, 1993): 64-84.

19. Frankenberg, *White Women.*

20. Joe Feagin. *The White Racial Frame*. (New York: Routledge, 2020).

21. Feagin, *The White Racial Frame.*

22. Victor Mather. "A Timeline of Colin Kaepernick vs. the N.F.L,. "*New York Times*, February 15, 2019. https://www.nytimes.com/2019/02/15/sports/nfl-colin-kaepernick -protests-timeline.html

23. DiAngelo, *What Does it Mean To Be White,* 143.

24. Brakkton Booker. "Roger Goodell On Colin Kaepernick's Possible Return to NFL: 'I Welcome That,'" *NPR*, June 16, 2020. https://www.npr.org/sections/live-updates -protests-for-racial-justice/2020/06/16/878810674/roger-goodell-on-colin -kaepernicks-possible-return-to-nfl-i-welcome-that

25. Richard Hughes. *Myths America Lives By: White Supremacy and the Stories That Give Us Meaning, Second Edition*. (Champaign, IL: University of Illinois Press, 2018):103,105. Hughes' reference to the fourth time of trial is based on Robert Bellah's book *The Broken Covenant*, in which he refers to the Founding of the U.S. as a nation, The Civil War and the 1960's as America's three times of trial.

26. Frankenberg, *White Women.*

27. Hitchcock. *White Veil.*

28. Admittedly with the rise of DNA testing and organizations like Ancestry.com, many white Americans are becoming interested in exploring their genealogical roots, but for the most part this search is disconnected from any awareness of distinct European cultures. Ironically, I mark the beginning of the interest of whites in their ancestry with the 1977 TV mini-series "Roots," which told the story of the ancestors of one African-American, Alex Haley.

29. The charge of "reverse racism" is discussed more fully in Chapter 10.

30. DiAngelo, *White Fragility.*

31. W.E.B. Du Bois. *The Souls of Black Folk.* New York: Penguin Books 1903/1995): 45.

32. Antonia Gramsci. *Prison Notebooks, Volume II.* Translated by Joseph Buttigieg. (New York: Columbia University Press, 1975).

33. Matthew Hughey. "Hegemonic Whiteness: Structure, Agency, Allegiance," in *The Construction of Whiteness*, edited by Stephen Middleton, David Roediger and Donald Shaffer (Jackson, MS: University of Mississippi Press, 2016): 213-214.

34. Hughey, "Hegemonic Whiteness."

35. To my father's credit, when he visited me a few months later, saw the work I was doing and met some of the young people with whom I was working, his mind and perspective began to change and began an ongoing dialogue between us. We never came to agreement on the value of my work as a career, but I always felt his respect after that.

36. Harris, "Whiteness," 1710.

37. Harris, "Whiteness," 1710-1715.

38. Harris, "Whiteness," 1713.

39. Harris, "Whiteness," 1716.

40. This history is further explored in Chapter 5.

41. Harris, "Whiteness," 1721.

42. In Chapter 7 I address the fallacy of racial colorblindness.

43. Alexander, *The New Jim Crow.*

44. David Roediger. *The Wages of Whiteness: Race and the Making of the American Working Class, Revised Edition.* (New York: Verso, 2007).

45. John Stapleford. "The Tortuous Journey: The Condition of Black America," *The Christian Scholars Review*, 37 no. 2 (2008): 231-251; William Darity and Kristen Mullen. *From Here to Equality: Reparations for Black Americans in the Twenty-First Century.* (Chapel Hill, NC: University of North Carolina Press, 2020).

46. Roediger, *Wages.*

47. "The Matrix." Directed by Lana Wachowski. Warner Brothers film, 1999.

48. Hughes. *Myths.*

49. Hughes, *Myths*, 19.

50. Hughes, *Myths*, 10.

51. Hughes, *Myths*, 10-11.

52. Robert Jensen. *The Heart of Whiteness*. (San Francisco: City Lights Books, 2005): 3-4.

53. Noliwe Rooks. *Cutting School: Privatization and the End of Public Education*. (New York: The New Press, 2017); White. "The Data are Damning."

54. Stapleford, "Torturous Journey;" Darity and Mullen, *From Here to Equality*.

55. Alexander, *The New Jim Crow*.

56. Edgar Villanueva. *Decolonizing Wealth: Indigenous Wisdom to Heal the Divides and Restore Bala*nce. (Oakland, CA: Berrett-Koehler Publishers, 2018): 24.

Chapter 4: How Racism Hurts White People

1. Wendell Berry. *The Hidden Wound*. (New York: North Point Press, 1989): 3-4.

2. James Tillman, *Why America Needs Racism and Poverty*. (Atlanta, GA: James and Mary Tillman, 1969): 39-40.

3. Tillman, *Why America*, 40.

4. Reesma Menakem. *My Grandmother's Hands: Racialized Trauma and the Pathway to Mending Our Hearts and Bodies*. (Las Vegas: Central Recovery Press, 2017).

5. Menakem, *Grandmother's Hands*, 39.

6. Joy DeGruy. *Post Traumatic Slave Syndrome: America's Legacy of Enduring Injury and Healing*. (Portland, OR: Joy DeGruy Publications, 2015): 121.

7. Menakem, *Grandmother's Hands*.

8. Kathleen Brown-Rice. "Examining the Theory of Historical Trauma Among Native Americans. *The Professional Counselor,* 3 no. 3 (2013):117-130. http://tpcjournal.nbcc.org/examining-the-theory-of-historical-trauma-among-native-americans/

9. Aaron Denham. "Rethinking Historical Trauma: Narratives of Resilience," *Transcultural Psychiatry,* 45 no. 3 (2008): 391-414.

10. Bernhard Giesen. "The Trauma of Perpetrators: The Holocaust as Traumatic Reference of German National Identity," in *Cultural Trauma and Collective Identity,* edited by Jeffrey C. Alexander et. al. (Berkeley, CA: University of California Press, 2004):112-154.

11. Becky Thompson and Veronica T. Watson. "Theorizing White Racial Trauma and Its Remedies," in *The Construction of Whiteness: An Interdisciplinary Analysis of Race Formation and the Meaning of White Identity,* edited by Stephen Middleton et. al. (Jackson, MS: University of Mississippi Press, 2016): 234-255.

12. Quoted in Daniel Hill. *White Awake*. (Downers Grove, IL: InterVarsity Press, 2017): 72.

13. Menakem, *Grandmother's Hands*, 4-5.

14. Nancy Isenberg. *White Trash: The 400 Year Untold History of Class in America*. (New York: Penguin Books, 2016).

15. Menakem, *Grandmother's Hands*, 61.

16. Examples of Irish riots against African Americans in the mid-19th century are recounted in Iver Bernstein, I. *The New York City Draft Riots: Their Significance for American Society and Politics in the Age of the Civil War*. (New York: Oxford University Press,1990); Daniel Biddle and Murray Dubin. *Tasting Freedom: Octavius Catto and the Battle for Equality in Civil War America*. (Philadelphia: Temple University Press, 2020).

17. DiAngelo, *White Fragility*.

18. Robin DiAngelo. "White Fragility," *International Journal of Critical Pedagogy*, 3 no. 3 (2011): 54.

19. The reptilian brain refers to the part of the brain just above the brain stem. It controls basic life functions such as breathing, body temperature and balance. It's also the place where the fight/flight/freeze response originates. The reptilian brain is reliable in protecting the person, but is rigid and undiscerning. See "The Brain". McGill University. https://thebrain.mcgill.ca/index.php.

20. This belief is validated by the disproportionate number of persons of color who work in the nursing care and home care professions caring for sick and ageing whites.

21. Menakem, *Grandmother's Hands*. 98-99.

22. Menakem, *Grandmother's Hands*, 98-101.

23. Menakem points out that the urge to soothe the white person's discomfort can be a self-protective strategy against white retaliation, but also serves to collude with white fragility and reinforce white privilege. In a sense this collusion can be likened to the enabling of an addict's addiction by the caretaker or friend.

24. Jonathan Metzl. *Dying of Whiteness: How the Politics of Racial Resentment Is Killing America's Heartland*. (New York: Basic Books, 2019).

25. Tillman. *Why America*.

26. We will explore some of Menakem's suggestions in ch. 9.

27. Stephen Covey. *The Seven Habits of Highly Effective People*. (New York: Simon and Schuster, 1989).

Chapter 5: Knowing Our Histories

1. Michelle Obama. "Transcript: Read Michelle Obama's full speech from the 2016 DNC," *CNN*, July 26, 2016. https://www.cnn.com/2016/07/26/politics/transcript-michelle -obama-speech-democratic-national-convention/index.html

2. Michelle Malkin tweet quoted in Callum Borchers. "How the Media covered Michelle Obama's 'House That Was Built by Slaves' Line," *Washington Post*, July 26, 2016. https://www.washingtonpost .com/news/the-fix/wp/2016/07/26/ how-the-media-covered-michelle-obamas-house-that-was-built-by-slaves-line/

3. Alexander Lane. "The Legend of Slaves Building Capitol is Correct," *Politifact*, January 19, 2009. https://www.politifact.com/factchecks/2009/jan/19/nancy-pelosi/legend -slaves-building-capitol-correct/

4. Louis Jacobsen. "Michelle Obama Correct That the White House Was Built By Slaves," *Politifact*. July 25, 2016. https://www.politifact.com/factchecks/2016/jul/25/

michelle-obama/michelle-obama-correct-white-house-was-built-slave/ ; Borchers "How the Media;" Daniel Victor. "Bill O'Reilly Defends Comments About 'Well Fed' Slaves,'" *The New York Times*, July 27, 2016. https://www.nytimes.com/ 2016/07/28/business/media/bill-oreilly-says-slaves-who-helped-build-white-house-were-well-fed.html

5. Dominique Morisseau. *Mud Row* (a play). Performed at the People's Light Theater, Malvern, PA, July 24, 2019.

6. Takaki, *A Different Mirror.*

7. Various organizations are dedicated to providing resources for schools and teachers on this untold and unrecognized dimension of U.S. history. Notable among these groups are the Zinn Education Project (https://www.zinnedproject.org/) and Rethinking Schools (https://www.rethinkingschools.org/).

8. Elizabeth Prine Pauls "Native American History," *Encyclopedia Britannica.* Accessed March 20, 2020 at https://www.britannica.com/topic/Native-American/Native -American-history

9. Roxanne Dunbar-Ortiz. *An Indigenous Peoples' History of the United States: ReVisioning American History.* (Boston: Beacon Press, 2014).

10. Some of the best resources for the history of racism include the following: George Frederickson. *Racism: A Short History.* (Princeton, NJ: Princeton University Press, 2002); Ibram X. Kendi. *Stamped From the Beginning: The Definitive History of Racist Ideas in America.* (New York: Nation Books, 2016); Audrey Smedley. *Race in North America: Origin and Evolution of a Worldview.* (Boulder CO: Westview Press, 2007).

11. Takaki *A Different Mirror.*

12. Editors of Encyclopedia Britannica. "Hydra – Greek Mythology." *Encyclopedia Britannica.* https://www.britannica.com/topic/Hydra-Greek-mythology

13. Frederick Douglass. "What to the Slave Is the Fourth of July?" in *Frederick Douglass, The Orator*, edited by James M. Gregory. (Sydney, Australia: Wentworth Press., 2019): 103-106.

14. Declaration of Independence. Accessed at http://www.ushistory.org/declaration/document/

15. Malik Simba. "The Three Fifths Clause of the United States Constitution (1787)," *Black Past*, October 3, 2014. https://www.Blackpast.org/african-american-history/three -fifths-clause-united-states-constitution-1787/

16. "The Nationality Act of 1790. *Immigration History*, The University of Texas at Austin, Department of History, 2019. https://immigrationhistory .org/item/1790-nationality-act/

17. The Treaty of Guadalupe Hidalgo transferred Mexican territory of what today is the American Southwest to the United States. Mexicans were given the right to be citizens if they decided to stay but had no rights to their property or ancestral lands. In order to keep their lands they had to prove to the courts that they could speak English. As a result many well-established Mexicans lost their land and rights, simply because the border moved.

18. Pat Griffin, Maurianne Adams and Lee Anne Bell. "History of Racism and Immigration Timeline," in *Teaching for Diversity and Social Justice, 2nd Edition.* (New York:

Routledge, 2007). http://www.racialequitytools.org/resourcefiles /racismimmigration-timeline.pdf

19. Dunbar-Ortiz, *Indigenous Peoples' History.*

20. Kendi. *Stamped.* All the insights, unless otherwise noted come from Kendi's book.

21. Kendi, *Stamped,* 3.

22. Kendi, *Stamped,* 9.

23. Roithmayr, *Reproducing Racism.*

24. Alexander, *New Jim Crow.*

25. Hughes, *Myths,* 3.

26. For a discussion of the persistence of racial segregation and inequalities in schools, see Sarah Mervosh. "How Much Wealthier are White School Districts Than Nonwhite Ones? $23 Billion Report Says." *New York Times* February 27, 2019. https://www.nytimes .com /2019/02/27/education/school-districts-funding-white-minorities.html?module =inline

27. Roithmayr, *Reproducing Racism.*

28. Alexander, *New Jim Crow.*

29. Adam Liptak and Michael Wines. "Strict North Carolina Voter ID Law Thwarted After Supreme Court Rejects Case," *New York Times,* May 15, 2017. https://www.nytimes .com/2017/05/15/ us/politics/voter-id-laws-supreme-court-north-carolina.html

30. Maggie Astor. "Seven Ways Alabama Has Made It Harder to Vote," *New York Times,* June 23, 2018. https://www.nytimes.com/2018/06/23/us/politics/voting-rights -alabama.html

31. Edwin Ball. *Slaves in my Family.* (New York: Farrar, Straus and Giroux, 1998).

32. History.com Editors. "Homestead Act," *The History Channel.* April 24, 2020. https:// www.history.com/topics/american-civil-war/homestead-act

33. Boyd. *White Allies.*

34. William Faulkner. *Requiem for a Nun.* (New York: Random House, 1950).

35. One organization that has helped both African American and white people trace their racial histories is Coming to the Table, which holds annual gatherings and provides resources to help people trace their racial history. Go to www. https://comingtothetable .org for more information.

Chapter 6: Start With Their Story and Listen: The Transformative Power of Dialogue

1. The Martin Luther King, Jr., Research and Education Institute, Stanford University. (2019). The Birmingham Campaign. Retrieved 1/24/20 at https://kinginstitute .stanford.edu/encyclopedia/birmingham-campaign

2. Michael Eric Dyson. *What Truth Sounds Like.* (New York: St. Martin's Press, 2018): 25.

3. Dyson, *Truth,* 28.

4. Dyson, *Truth,* 38.

5. Dyson, *Truth,* 39.

6. Dyson, *Truth,* 40.

7. Dyson, *Truth,* 43.

8. Dyson, *Truth,* 47.

9. Dyson, *Truth,* 51, 52.

10. Dyson, *Truth,* 16-17.

11. Dyson, *Truth,* 48.

12. I discuss confronting overt racism in ch. 12.

13. This section on the history and methodology of NewCORE comes from a conversation with Rev. Dr. Steven Lawrence, asst. to the pastor, White Rock Baptist Church (Philadelphia, PA) and president of NewCORE on April 9, 2019.

14. For more information on NewCORE, go to https://newcorephilly.org/

15. Parker Palmer. *A Hidden Wholeness: The Journey Toward the Undivided Life.* (San Francisco: Jossey-Bass, 2004):132-134.

16. Colin Bridges. "Telling Stories: Past and Present Heroes," *Frontiers: The Interdisciplinary Journal of Study Abroad XIV,* 2007: 32.

17. Covey. *Habits,* 235.

18. Covey, *Habits,* 239.

19. Covey, *Habits.*

20. This section is largely informed by two sources. Ira Shor and Paulo Freire, *A Pedagogy for Liberation: Dialogues on Transforming Education.* (Westport, CT: Bergin and Garvey, 1987); Paulo Freire, *Pedagogy of the Oppressed, 30th Anniversary Edition.* (New York: Continuum, 2007).

21. Shor and Freire, *Pedagogy,* 100.

22. Greg Ellison. *Fearless Dialogues: A New Movement for Justice.* (Louisville, KY: Westminster John Knox Press, 2017).

23. Megan Boler and Michalanos Zembylas. "Discomforting Truths: The Emotional Terrain of Understanding Difference," in *Pedagogies of Difference: Rethinking Education for Social Change,* edited Peter Pericles Trifonis. (New York: Routledge, 2003): 116-139.

24. Boler and Zembylas, "Discomforting Truths."

25. Ellison, *Fearless Dialogues,* 13.

26. Freire, *Pedagogy of the Oppressed,* 90.

27. Paulo Freire. *Pedagogy of Hope: Reliving Pedagogy of the Oppressed.* (New York: Continuum, 1996).

28. Freire, *Pedagogy of the Oppressed,* 88.

29. Freire, *Pedagogy of the Oppressed,* Note #15, p. 99.

30. Paulo Freire. *Teachers as Cultural Workers: Letters to Those Who Dare to Teach.* (Boulder, CO: Westview Press, 1998): 42.

31. Freire, *Teachers*, 42.

Chapter 7: Responding to Claims of Colorblindness

1. Katherine Tarca. "Colorblind in Control: The Risks of Resisting Differences Amid Demographic Change," *Educational Studies*, 38 no. 2, (2015): 100.

2. Frederick Herzog. "Black and White Together?" *Duke Divinity School Review*, 34 no. 2 (1969): 120.

3. Laura G. Babbitt, Negan R. Toosi and Samuel R. Sommers. "A Broad and Insidious Appeal: Unpacking the Reasons for Endorsing Racial Color Blindness," in *The Myth of Racial Colorblindness: Manifestations, Dynamics and Impact*, edited by Helen A. Neville, Miguel E. Gallardo and Derald Wing Sue. (Washington, DC: American Psychological Association, 2016): 53-68.

4. Eduardo Bonilla-Silva. *Racism Without Racists: Color-Blind Racism and the Persistence of Racial Inequality in America, 4th Edition.* (New York: Rowman and Littlefield Publishers, 2014).

5. Lopez. *Dog Whistle Politics.*

6. The Southern Strategy was first developed by Kevin Phillips a staffer in the Nixon administration that sought to play on southern disdain for African Americans. One could argue that with the presidency of Donald Trump racist rhetoric has increased and has led to re-emergence of white nationalism in the U.S. Pres. Trump's is less subtle when he refers to African nations as "shithole countries," specifically criticizes female Congresswomen of color when they criticize him, or refers to white nationalist marching in Charlottesville as "good people." Even so he likes to refer to himself as the "least racist person in the world" and touts the low unemployment rate among African Americans and does not publicly use overtly racist terms only code words. See Dov Grohsgal and Kevin M. Kruse. "How the Republican Majority Emerged," *The Atlantic*, August 6, 2019. https://www.theatlantic.com/ideas/archive/2019/08/emerging-republican-majority/595504/.

7. Ironically President Donald Trump in his quest for re-election in 2020, has chosen to use a more direct appeal white racial fears and racist stereotypes. See Peter Baker. "More Than Ever, Trump Casts Himself as the Defender of White America," *New York Times*, September 6, 2020. https://nyti.ms/2FbTrsB

8. Bonilla-Silva. *Racism.*

9. Bonilla-Silva. *Racism*, 3.

10. Bonilla-Silva. *Racism*, 4.

11. Bonilla-Silva. *Racism.*

12. Jennifer C. Mueller. "Producing Colorblindness: Everyday Mechanisms of White Ignorance," *Social Problems*, 64 no. 2 (2017): 219-238.

13. James Jones. "The Color-Blind Racial Approach: Does Race Really Matter?" in *The Myth of Racial Colorblindness: Manifestations, Dynamics and Impact*, edited by Helen A.

Neville, Miguel E. Gallardo, and Derald Wing Sue. (Washington, DC: American Psychological Association, 2016): 39-52.

14. Eduardo Bonilla-Silva. "The Linguistics of Color Blind Racism: How to Talk Nasty About Blacks Without Sounding 'Racist,'" *Critical Sociology*, 28 nos. 1-2), 2002: 41-64.; and Eduardo Bonilla-Silva. "The Invisible Weight of Whiteness: The Racial Grammar of Everyday Life in Contemporary America," *Ethnic and Racial Studies*, 35 no. 2 (2012): 173-194.

Chapter 8: Guilt, Shame and Denial

1. Beverly Tatum. *Why Are All the Black Kids Sitting Together in the Cafeteria? And Other Conversations About Race.* (New York: Perseus Books, 1997).

2. Hitchcock. *White Veil.*

3. Aarti Iyer, Colin Wayne Leach and Faye Crosby. "White Guilt and Racial Compensation: The Benefits and Limits of Self-Focus," *Personality and Social Psychology Bulletin*, 29 no. 1 (2005): 118.

4. See Chapter 2.

5. Shelby Steele. *White Guilt: How Blacks and Whites Together Destroyed the Promise of the Civil Rights Era.* (New York: Harper/Perennial, 2006).

6. Peter Grzanka. *White Guilt: Race, Gender, Sexuality and Emergent Racism in the Contemporary United States.* PhD. Diss. University of Maryland College Park, 2020.

7. Janet Helms. "Toward a Model of White Racial Identity Development," in *Black and White Racial Identity: Theory, Research and Practice*, edited by Janet Helms. (Westport, CT: Praeger Publishers, 1990): 49-66; and Tatum, *Black Kids*, 93-113.

8. Helms, "Toward a Model," 58.

9. Helms, "Toward a Model," 96.

10. Quoted Tatum, *Black Kids,* 101.

11. Helms, "Toward a Model," 62.

12. Tatum, *Black Kids*, 103.

13. Ironically those same whites will use the idea of whites as a collective when they oppose policies like affirmative action as "discrimination against whites." See Chapter 10.

14. Brene Brown. *Daring Greatly: How the Courage to Be Vulnerable Transforms the Way We Live, Love, Parent and Lead.* (New York: Penguin, 2012).

15. Brown, *Daring*, 68-69.

16. Thandeka (1999*). Learning to be White.* (New York: Continuum/Bloomsbury Academic, 1999).

17. James Baldwin. "The White Man's Guilt, " in *James Baldwin: Collected Essays*, edited by Toni Morrison. (New York: Literary Classics of the United States, 1998): 722-727.

18. Gary Howard. "White Man Dancing," in *Becoming and Unbecoming White: Owning and Disowning a Racial Identity,* edited by Christine Clark and James O'Donnell. (Westport, CT: Bergin and Garvey, 1999): 217.

19. Howard's most extensive discussion on racism in education is Gary Howard. *We Can't Teach What We Don't Know: White Teachers, Multiracial Schools*. (New York: Teachers College, 2006).

20. Faith Karimi. "Rachel Dolezal, White Woman Who Portrayed Herself as Black, Accused of Welfare Fraud." *CNN*, May 25, 2018. https://www.cnn.com/2018/05/25/us/rachel-dolezal-welfare-fraud-allegations/index.html

21. Hitchcock, *White Veil*.

22. Hill. *White Awake*, 68.

23. Hill, *White Awake*, 69.

24. Brett Russell Coleman, Courtney M. Bonham and Caitlyn Yantis. "'I Thought Ghettos Just Happened': White Americans' Responses to Learning About Placed-Based Critical History," in *History and Collective Memory from the Margins: A Global Perspective*, edited by Sahana Mukherjee and Phia Salter. (Hauppauge, NY: Nova Science Publishers, 2019): 1-22

25. Hill, *White Awake*, 71-72

26. Baldwin, "Guilt," 725.

27. Kendi, *Antiracist*.

28. Howard, "White Man Dancing," 218.

29. Howard, "White Man Dancing."

30. Kendi, *Antiracist*.

31. Kendi, *Antiraci*st, 235.

32. Helms, "Toward a Model."

33. Tatum, *Black Kids*, 112-113.

34. I wrote my book *White Allies in the Struggle for Racial Justice* (Orbis, 2015) to illustrate how some deeply flawed and racist white people, through hard work and deep self-reflection, became allies in the cause for racial justice in their time.

35. Baldwin, "Guilt," 722.

36. DiAngelo, *White Fragility*.

37. DiAngelo, *White Fragility*.

Chapter 9: Fears, Tears and Anger

1. Kendi, *Antiracist*, 325.

2. Antoine J. Banks. *Anger and Racial Politics: The Emotional Foundation of Racial Attitudes in America*. (New York: Cambridge University Press, 2014): 8.

3. Howard, "White Man Dancing," 213. .

4. Howard, "White Man Dancing," 213.

5. Dana Ford. "Juror: 'No Doubt" that George Zimmerman Feared for His Life," *CNN*, July 16, 2013. https://www.cnn.com/2013/07/15/justice/zimmerman-juror-book/index.html

6. Martenzie Johnson. "Joe McKnight and the Fear of the Black Man," *The Undefeated*, December 5, 2016. https://theundefeated.com/features/joe-mcknight-and-the-fear-of-the-Black-man/

7. U. S. Department of Justice. *Department of Justice Report Regarding the Criminal Investigation into the Shooting of Michael Brown by Ferguson Missouri Police Officer Darren Wilson*, March 4, 2015. https://www.justice.gov/sites/default/files/opa/press-releases/attachments/2015/03/04/ doj_report_on_shooting_of_michael_brown_1. pdf

8. Jose A. Del Real. "No Charges in Sacramento Police Shooting of Stephon Clark," *New York Times*, March 4, 2019. https://www.nytimes.com/2019/03/02/us/stephon-clark-police-shooting-sacramento.html

9. DiAngelo, *White Fragility*, 105.

10. Menakem, *Grandmother's Hands*.

11. James Douglas Rice. "Bacon's Rebellion (1676-1677)," *Encyclopedia Virginia*, (no date). https://www.encyclopediavirginia.org/bacon_s_rebellion_1676-1677#start_entry

12. John Elrick. "The Impact of the Haitian Revolution on the United States: An Historiographical Essay," *San Francisco State, Department of History*, XIX, Spring 2010. https://history.sfsu.edu/sites/default/files/EPF/ 2010_John%20Elrick.pdf; Ann Hagedorn. *Beyond the River: The Untold Story of the Heroes of the Underground Railroad*. (New York: Simon and Schuster, 2002): 18-20.

13. Banks, *Anger*, 37.

14. The reason for school segregation today is due to increased residential segregation, as opposed to mandated Black and white schools, but the overall effect is the same. See Jason M. Breslow, Evan Wexler and Robert Collins. "The Return of School Segregation in Eight Charts," *Frontline*, July 15, 2014. https://www.pbs.org/wgbh/frontline/article/the-return-of-school-segregation-in-eight-charts/

15. DiAngelo, *White Fragility*, 111.

16. George E. Curry. "Pat Buchanan Explains White Fears Over Diversity. *The Chicago Crusader*, May 16, 2016. https://chicagocrusader.com/pat-buchanan-explains-white-fears-diversity/

17. Hui Bai and Christopher Frederico. "Collective Existential Threat Mediates White population Decline's Effect on Defensive Reactions," *Group Process and Intergroup relations*, 23 no. 23 (2019): 361-377.

18. DiAngelo, *White Fragility*.

19. DiAngelo, *White Fragility*.

20. Sarita Srivastava. "Tears, Fears and Careers: Anti-Racism and Emotion in Social Movement Organizations," *Canadian Journal of Sociology*, 31 no. 1 (2006): 55-90.

21. Srivastava, "Tears," 61.

22. DiAngelo, *White Fragility*, 132.

23. Michael Kimmel. *Angry White Men: American Masculinity at the End of an Era*. (New York: Perseus Book Group, 2017).

24. Kimmel, *Angry*, 4.

25. Tristan Bridges. "Angry White Men: A Book Review," *Huffington Post*, March 18, 2014. https://www.huffpost.com/entry/a-review-of-angry-white-m_b_4611216

26. Bridges "Angry."

27. Todd C. Frankel. "Gun Sales Spiked After Ferguson Unrest: Will Gun Crime Rise As Well?" *Washington Post,* January 7, 2015. https://www.washingtonpost.com/news/storyline/wp/2015/01/07/guns-sales-spiked-after-the-ferguson-unrest-will-gun-crime-rise-as-well/

28. Kathleen E. Carey. "Black Lives Matter Turns Tense in Ridley Township," *The Delco Times*, August 2, 2020. https://www.delcotimes.com/news/Black-lives-matter-march-turns-tense-in-ridley-township/article_c612917a-d43c-11ea-befb-934f56f1aa53.html

29. Menakem, *Grandmother's Hands*.

30. Menakem, *Grandmother's Hands*, 129.

31. Menakem, *Grandmother's Hands,* 130.

32. Howard Stevenson. *Promoting Racial Literacy in Schools: Differences That Make a Difference*. (New York: Teachers College Press, 2014).

33. Stevenson, *Racial Literacy*, 126-127.

34. Stevenson, *Racial Literacy,* 127.

35. News One Staff. "Let's Not Forget When Joe Biden Called Obama 'Articulate' and 'Clean' and Said It Was Taken Out of Context," *News One*, June 28, 2019. https://newsone.com/3881474/joe-biden-obama-articulate-clean-context/.

36. Antje Mattheus and LorraineMarino. "Guidelines for Giving Effective Feedback," *White People Confronting Racism*. (Antje Mattheus and Lorraine Marino, 2011): 70.

Chapter 10: Uncovering the Lie of Reverse Racism

1. See Chapter 3.

2. National Public Radio. "Stories on Racial Disparities." https://www.npr.org/tags/371446041/racial-disparities. Numerous other studies are put out regularly by Pew Research Center and the Urban League.

3. Nolan Cabrera. "'The Only Racism Left Is That Against White People': The Complex Realities of the Campus Racial Climate for Latina/o Students," in *Hispanic College Students Moving Forward: Policies, Planning and Progress in Promoting Access*, edited by Alfred G. de los Santos et. al. (Tempe, AZ: Bilingual Press, 2017): 275-290.

4. Nolan Cabrera. "'But I'm Oppressed Too'": White Male College Students Framing Racial Emotions and Recreating Racism," *International Journal of Qualitative Studies in Education,* 27 no. 6 (2014): 768-784.

5. Stanley Fish. "Reverse Racism, or How the Pot Got to Call the Kettle Black," *The Atlantic*, November 1993. https://www.theatlantic.com/magazine/archive/1993/11/reverse-racism-or-how-the-pot-got-to-call-the-kettle-Black/304638/

6. Cabrera, "Oppressed," 781.

7. Michael I. Norton and Samuel R. Sommers. "Whites See Racism as a Zero-Sum Game That They Are Now Losing," *Perspectives on Psychological Science,* 6 no. 3 (2011): 215-218.

8. Kendi, *Antiracist.*

9. Courtland Milloy. "How American Oligarchs Created the Concept of Race to Divide and Conquer the Poor," *Washington Post*, April 19, 2016. https://www.washingtonpost .com/local/how-wealthy-americans-divided-and-conquered-the-poor-to-create-the -concept-of-race/2016/04/19/2cab6e38-0643-11e6-b283-e79d81c63c1b_story .html

10. Peter Baker. "More Than Ever."

11. See Chapter 3.

12. Nolan, "Oppressed," 781.

13. Nolan, "Oppressed," 781.

14. See Chapters 4 & 9 on the effects of historic trauma on whites.

15. Barack Obama. "A More Perfect Union," delivered at the National Constitution Center, Philadelphia, PA, March 18, 2008. https://www.nytimes.com/2008/03/18/us/ politics/18text-obama.html

16. John Quinones' show "What Would You Do" covers a number of issues including racial discrimination, in everyday events in American life. A collection of his stories can be found on YouTube. These can be found at the official channel for "What Would You Do" at https://www.youtube.com/channel/UCwdo8-3UrfZ9scHPl0m4Ysg

17. The tactic of divide and conquer that sets low income whites and BIPOC against each other is discussed in Chapter 4. See Note 314.

Chapter 11: White Liberals

1. Mark Warren. *Fire in the Heart: How White Activists Embrace Racial Justice.* (New York: Oxford University Press, 2014):19.

2. Warren, *Fire.*

3. Shannon Sullivan. *Good White People: The Problem with Middle-Class White Anti-Racism.* (Albany, NY: SUNY Press, 2014).

4. Isaac Chotiner. "Why White Liberals Are So Unwilling to Recognize Their Own Racism," *Slate*, August 2, 2018. https://slate.com/news-and-politics/2018/08/white-liberal -racism-why-progressives-are-unable-to-see-their-own-bigotry.html

5. Zak Foste. "The Enlightenment Narrative: White Student Leaders' Preoccupation with Racial Innocence," *Journal of Diversity in Higher Education,* 13 no. 1 (2020):33-43.

6. Shelly Tochluk. *Witnessing Whiteness: The Need to Talk About Race and How to Do It, Second Edition.* (Lanham, MD: Rowman & Littlefield Education, 2010).

7. Cydney Dupree and Susan T. Fiske. "Self-Presentation in Interracial Settings: The Competence Downshift by White Liberals," *Journal of Personality and Social Psychology: Interpersonal Relations and Group Processes*, 117 no. 3 (2019): 579-604.

8. Solomon Jones. "Facing Up to Racism of White Liberals," *Philadelphia Inquirer*, December 4, 2018. https://www.inquirer.com/columnists/yale-study-white-liberals-Black-conversation-solomon-jones-20181204.html

9. Quoted in Sullivan, *Good White People*, 22.

10. Jordan Flaherty. *No More Heroes: Grassroots Challenges to the Savior Mentality*. (Chico, CA: AK Press, 2016).

11. Flaherty. *No More Heroes*, 2.

12. Flaherty. *No More Heroes*, 50.

13. Flaherty. *No More Heroes*, 56.

14. Flaherty. *No More Heroes*.

15. Hitchcock. *White Veil*, 199.

16. Flaherty. *No More Heroes*, 13-14.

17. Freire. *Pedagogy of the Oppressed*.

18. Freire. *Pedagogy of the Oppressed*, 135.

19. Freire. *Pedagogy of the Oppressed*, 61.

20. For a fuller discussion Freire's idea of "conversion to the people," see James Kirylo and Drick Boyd. *Paulo Freire: His Faith, Spirituality and Theology*. (Rotterdam: Sense Publishing, 2017): 13-26.

Chapter 12: Interrupting Overt Racism

1. *Speak Up: Responding to Everyday Bigotry*. Southern Poverty Law Center. (2015):77. www.splcenter.org/20150125/speak-responding-everyday-bigotry

2. *Speak Up*, 77.

3. Author interview with Tim Wise, November 13, 2013.

4. I have added the concept of staying connected to what was printed in the SPLC document.

5. Michael Kerr and Murray Bowen. *Family Evaluation: An Approach Based on Bowen Theory*. (New York: W.W. Norton & Company, 1988): 145, footnote #7.

6. Edwin Friedman. *Generation to Generation: Family Process in Church and Synagogue*. (New York: Guilford Press, 1985): 228-230.

7. *Speak Up*, 79.

8. Janelle Griffith. "Man Sent Anti-Muslim Tweets to a Political Candidate Who Then Helped Pay His Medical Debt," *NBC News*, March 10, 2020. https://www.nbcnews.com/news/us-news/man-sent-anti-muslim-tweets-political-candidate-who-then-helped-n1154581.

Chapter 13: Relentless Responsibility

1. Michael Eric Dyson. *Tears We Cannot Stop: A Sermon to White America*. (New York: St. Martin's Press, 2017): 44.

2. Dyson, *Tears*, 49.

3. Baldwin, "Guilt," 723.

4. Jennifer Harvey. *Dear White Christians: For Those Still Longing for Racial Reconciliation.* (Grand Rapids, MI: William B. Eerdmans, 2014): 56.

5. Abraham Joshua Heschel. "Religion and Race," in *Abraham Joshua Heschel: Essential Writings*, edited by Suzanna Heschel. (Maryknoll, NY: Orbis Books, 2011): 65-75.

6. Heschel, "Religion and Race," 65.

7. Maya Angelou. "Equality," in *Maya Angelou: The Complete Poetry.* (New York: Random House, 2015): 226.

1. Lopez, *Dog Whistle Politics.*

2. Mary McCullough. "CDC reports nearly 300,000 'excess deaths' this year. *Philadelphia Inquirer*, October 21, 2020. https://www.inquirer.com/health/coronavirus/live/covid-coronavirus-cases-pa-philadelphia-nj-de-updates-testing-news-20201020.html

3. John Kania and Liz Weaver. "People, Practice and Transformational Change," Tamarack Institute Webinar, October 21, 2020. Online

4. Maurice Chammah and Cary Aspinwall. "The Short, Fraught History of the 'Thin Blue Line' American Flag," The Marshall Project, March 8, 2020. https://www.themarshallproject.org/2020/06/08/the-short-fraught-history-of-the-thin-blue-line-american-flag

5. Kania and Weaver, "People."

References

Adams, Maurianne, Lee Anne Bell and Pat Griffin. "History of Racism and Immigration Time-line," *Teaching for Diversity and Social Justice, 2nd Edition*. Routledge 2007. http://www.racialequitytools.org/resourcefiles/racismimmigration-timeline.pdf

Alexander, Michelle. *The New Jim Crow: Mass Incarceration in the Age of Colorblindness*. New York: The New Press, 2009.

Angelou, Maya. "Equality," in *Maya Angelou: The Complete Poetry*, 226. New York: Random House, 2015.

Associated Press. "House Rebukes GOP's Steve King Over Racist Remarks," *New York Times*, January 15, 2019. https://apnews.com/712ea1e8c9f24f8ba3afd7b680288a87l

Astor, Maggie. "Seven Ways Alabama Has Made It Harder to Vote," *New York Times*, June 23, 2018. https://www.nytimes.com/2018/06/23/us/politics/voting-rights-alabama.html

Babbitt, Laura, Negin Toosi and Samuel Sommers. "A Broad and Insidious Appeal: Unpacking the Reasons for Endorsing Racial Color Blindness," in *The Myth of Racial Color Blindness: Manifestations, Dynamics and Impact*, edited by Helen Neville, Miguel Gallardo and Derald Wing Sue, 53-68. Washington, DC: American Psychological Association, 2016.

Bai, Hui and Christopher Frederico. "Collective Existential Threat Mediates White Population Decline's Effect on Defensive Reactions," *Group Process and Intergroup Relations*, 23 no. 3 (2020): 361-377.

Baker, Peter. "More Than Ever, Trump Casts Himself as the Defender of White America," *New York Times*, September 6, 2020. https://nyti.ms/2FbTrsB

Baldwin, James. "The White Man's Guilt," in *James Baldwin: Collected Essays,* edited by Toni Morrison, 722-727. New York: Literary Classics of the United States, 1998.

Ball, Edwin. *Slaves in My Family*. New York: Farrar, Straus and Giroux, 1998.

Banks, Antoine. *Anger and Racial Politics: The Emotional Foundation of Racial Attitudes in America*. New York: Cambridge University Press, 2014.

Bazelon, Emily. "White People Are Noticing Something New: Their Own Whiteness," *New York Times*, June 13, 2018. https://www.nytimes.com/2018/06/13/magazine/white-people-are-noticing-something-new-their-own-whiteness.html

Bernstein, Iver. *The New York City Draft Riots: Their Significance for American Society and Politics in the Age of the Civil War*. New York: Oxford University Press, 1990.

Berry, Wendell. *The Hidden Wound*. New York: North Point Press, 1989.

Berry-Jester, Anna Marie. "Attitudes Toward Racism and Inequality Are Shifting," *ABC News*, June 23, 2015. https://fivethirtyeight.com/features/attitudes-toward-racism-and -inequality-are-shifting/

Biddle, Daniel and Murray Dubin. *Tasting Freedom: Octavius Catto and the Battle for Equality in Civil War America*. Philadelphia: Temple University Press, 2010.

Boler, Megan and Michalinos Zembylas. "Discomforting Truths: The Emotional Terrain of Understanding Difference," in *Pedagogies of Difference: Rethinking Education for Social Change*, edited by Peter Pericles Trifonis, 116-139. New York: Routledge, 2003.

Bonilla-Silva, Eduardo. "The Linguistics of Color Blind Racism: How to Talk Nasty About Blacks Without Sounding 'Racist,'" *Critical Sociology*, 28 nos. 1-2 (2002): 41-64.

Bonilla-Silva, Eduardo. "The Invisible Weight of Whiteness: The Racial Grammar of Everyday Life in Contemporary America," *Ethnic and Racial Studies*, 35 no. 2 (2012): 173-194.

Bonilla-Silva, Eduardo. *Racism Without Racists: Color-Blind Racism and the Persistence of Racial Inequality in America, 4th Edition*. New York: Rowman and Littlefield Publishers, 2014.

Booker, Brakkton. "Roger Goodell on Colin Kaepernick's Possible Return to NFL: 'I Welcome That,'" *NPR*, June 16, 2020. https://www.npr.org/sections/live-updates-protests-for -racial-justice/2020/06/16/878810674/roger-goodell-on-colin-kaepernicks-possible -return-to-nfl-i-welcome-that

Borchers, Callum. "How the Media Covered Michelle Obama's 'House That Was Built by Slaves' Line," *Washington Post*, July 26, 2016. https://www.washingtonpost.com/ news/the-fix/wp/2016/07/26/how-the-media-covered-michelle-obamas-house-that -was-built-by-slaves-line

Boyd, Drick. "Autoethnography as a Tool for Transformative Learning About White Privilege," *Journal of Transformative Education*, 6 no. 3 (2008): 212-225.

Boyd, Drick. *White Allies in the Struggle for Racial Justice*. Maryknoll, NY: Orbis, 2015.

Bridges, Tristan. "Angry White Men: A Book Review," *Huffington Post*, March 18, 2014. https://www.huffpost.com/entry/a-review-of-angry-white-m_b_4611216

Brooking Institute. "The U.S. Will Become 'Minority White' in 2045," *Census Projects: Youthful Minorities Are the Engine of Future Growth*, 2018. https://www.brookings.edu /blog/the-avenue/2018/03/14/ the-us-will-become-minority-white-in-2045-census-projects/

Brown, Brene. *Daring Greatly: How the Courage to Be Vulnerable Transforms the Way We Live, Love, Parent and Lead*. New York: Penguin, 2012.

Brown-Rice, Kathleen. "Examining the Theory of Historical Trauma Among Native Americans," *The Professional Counselor*, 3 no. 3 (2013): 117-130. http://tpcjournal.nbcc .org/examining-the-theory-of-historical-trauma-among-native-americans/

Cabrera, Nolan. "'But I'm Oppressed Too': White Male College Students Framing Racial Emotions and Recreating Racism," *International Journal of Qualitative Studies in Education*, 27 no. 6 (2014): 768-784.

Cabrera, Nolan. "'The Only Racism Left Is That Against White People': The Complex Realities of the Campus Racial Climate for Latina/o Students," in *Hispanic College Students Moving Forward: Policies, Planning and Progress in Promoting Access*, edited by Alfred G. de los Santos, Jr, Laura I. Rendon, Gary Francisco Keller, Alberto Acereda, Estele Mara Bensimon and Richard J. Tannenbaum, 275-290. Tempe, AZ: Bilingual Press, 2017.

Carey, Kathleen E. "Black Lives Matter Turns Tense in Ridley Township," *The Delco Times,* August 2, 2020. https://www.delcotimes.com/news/Black-lives-matter-march-turns -tense-in-ridley-township/article_c612917a-d43c-11ea-befb-934f56f1aa53.html

Centers for Disease Control and Prevention (CDC). "History of the 1918 Flu Pandemic." https://www.cdc.gov/flu/pandemic-resources/1918-commemoration/1918-pandemic -history.htm

Chotiner, Isaac. "Why White Liberals Are So Unwilling to Recognize Their Own Racism," *Slate,* August 2, 2018. https://slate.com/news-and-politics/2018/08/white-liberal -racism-why-progressives-are-unable-to-see-their-own-bigotry.html

Clark, M. Carolyn. "Narrative Learning: Its Contours and Its Possibilities," *New Directions for Adult and Continuing Education,* 126 (Summer 2010): 3-11.

Coleman, Brett Russell, Courtney M. Bonham and Caitlyn Yantis. "'I Thought Ghettos Just Happened': White Americans' Responses to Learning About Placed-Based Critical History," in *History and Collective Memory from the Margins: A Global Perspective*, edited by Sahana Mukherjee and Phia Salter, 1-22. Hauppauge, NY: Nova Science Publishers, 2019.

Covey, Stephen. *The Seven Habits of Highly Effective People*. New York: Simon and Schuster, 1989.

Curry, George E. "Pat Buchanan Explains White Fears Over Diversity, "*The Chicago Crusader.* May 16, 2016. https://chicagocrusader.com/pat-buchanan-explains-white-fears -diversity

Darity Jr., William A. and Kristen Mullen. *From Here to Equality: Reparations for Black Americans in the Twenty-First Century*. Chapel Hill, NC: The University of North Carolina Press, 2020.

DeGruy, Joy. *Post Traumatic Slave Syndrome: America's Legacy of Enduring Injury and Healing*. Portland, OR: Joy DeGruy Publications, 2005.

Delgado, Richard and Jean Stefanic. *Critical Race Theory: An Introduction*. New York: New York University Press, 2012.

Del Real, Jose. "No Charges in Sacramento Police Shooting of Stephon Clark," *New York Times*, March 4, 2019. https://www.nytimes.com/2019/03/02/us/stephon-clark -police-shooting-sacramento.html

Denham, Aaron R. "Rethinking Historical Trauma: Narratives of Resilience," *Transcultural Psychiatry* 45, no. 3 (2008): 391-414.

DiAngelo, Robin. "White Fragility," *International Journal of Critical Pedagogy*, 3 no. 3 (2011): 54-70.

DiAngelo, Robin. *What Does it Mean to Be White, Revised Edition.* New York: Peter Lang, 2016.

DiAngelo, Robin. *White Fragility: Why It's So Hard for White People to Talk About Racism.* Boston: Beacon Press, 2018.

DiAngelo, Robin. "White Fragility American Tour" (with Jack Hill). Friends Central School, Philadelphia, PA, April 17, 2019.

Donaghue, Erin. "2,120 Hate Incidents Against Asian Americans Reported During Coronavirus Pandemic," CBS News, July 2, 2020. https://www.cbsnews.com/news/anti-asian -american-hate-incidents-up-racism/

Douglass, Frederick. "What to the Slave is the Fourth of July?" in *Frederick Douglass, the Orator*, edited by James M. Gregory, 103-106. New York: Wentworth Press, 2017.

Du Bois, W.E.B. *The Souls of Black Folk.* New York: Penguin Books, 1995.

Du Bois, W.E.B. "The Souls of White People," in *Darkwater: Voices from Within the Veil.* Mineola, NY: Dover Publications,1999: 17-29.

Dunbar-Ortiz, Roxanne. *An Indigenous Peoples' History of the United States: ReVisioning American History.* Boston: Beacon Press, 2014.

Dupree, Cydney H. and Susan T. Fiske. "Self-Presentation in Interracial Settings: The Competence Downshift by White Liberals," *Journal of Personality and Social Psychology: Interpersonal Relations and Group Processes*, 117 no. 3 (2019): 579-604.

Dyson, Michael Eric. *Tears We Cannot Stop: A Sermon to White America.* New York: St. Martin's Press, 2017.

Dyson, Michael Eric. *What Truth Sounds Like.* New York: St. Martin's Press, 2018.

Ellison II, Greg C. *Fearless Dialogues: A New Movement for Justice.* Louisville, KY: Westminster John Knox Press, 2017.

Elrick, John. "The Impact of the Haitian Revolution on the United States: An Historiographical Essay," *Ex Post Facto: Journal of History Students at San Francisco State University.* XIX (Spring 2010). https://history.sfsu.edu/sites/dBeyond the river.efault/files/ EPF/ 2010_John%20Elrick.pdf

Feagin, Joe. *The White Racial Frame.* New York: Routledge, 2020.

Fish, Stanley. "Reverse Racism, or How The Pot Got to Call the Kettle Black," *The Atlantic,* November 1993. https://www.theatlantic.com/magazine/archive /1993/11/reverse -racism-or-how-the-pot-got-to-call-the-kettle-black/304638/

Flaherty, Jordan. *No More Heroes: Grassroots Challenges to the Savior Mentality.* Chicago: AK Press, 2016.

Dana, Ford. "Juror: 'No Doubt' that George Zimmerman Feared for His Life," *CNN,* July 16, 2013. https://www.cnn.com/2013/07/15/justice/zimmerman-juror-book/index.html

Foreman, Tyrone and Amanda E. Lewis. "Beyond Prejudice? Young Whites' Racial Attitudes in Post-Civil Rights America, 1976-2000," *American Behavioral Scientist*, 59 no. 11 (2015): 1394-1428.

Foste, Zak. "The Enlightenment Narrative: White Student Leaders' Preoccupation with Racial Innocence," *Journal of Diversity in Higher Education*, 13 no. 1 (2020): 33-43.

Frankel, Todd C. "Gun Sales Spiked After Ferguson Unrest: Will Gun Crime Rise As Well?" *Washington Post*, January 7, 2015. https://www.washingtonpost.com/news/ storyline/wp /2015/01/07/ guns-sales-spiked-after-the-ferguson-unrest-will-gun-crime-rise-as-well/

Frankenberg, Ruth. *White Women, Race Matters: The Social Construction of Whiteness*. Minneapolis, MN: University of Minnesota Press, 1993.

Frankenberg, Ruth. "White Women, Race Matters: The Social Construction of Whiteness," in *Critical Whiteness Studies: Looking Behind the Mirror*, edited by Richard Delgado and Jean Stefancic, 632-634. Philadelphia: Temple University Press, 1997.

Franson, Craig and Charles Gallagher. "Why All the Hate? White Supremacy, White Nationalism and White Power," La Salle University Digital Commons, 2019. https:// digitalcommons.lasalle.edu /explorercafe/84

Frederickson, George. *Racism: A Short History.* Princeton, NJ: Princeton University Press, 2002.

Freire, Paulo. *Pedagogy of the Oppressed, 30th Anniversary Edition*. New York: Continuum, 2007.

Freire, Paulo. *Pedagogy of Hope: Reliving Pedagogy of the Oppressed*. New York: Continuum, 1996.

Freire, Paulo. *Teachers as Cultural Workers: Letters to Those Who Dare to Teach*. Boulder, CO: Westview Press, 1998.

Friedman, Edwin. *Generation to Generation: Family Process in Church and Synagogue*. New York: Guilford Press, 1985.

Trip, Gabriel. "A Timeline of Steve King's Racist Remarks and Divisive Actions," *New York Times,* January 15, 2019. https://www.nytimes.com/2019/01/15/us/politics/steve -king-offensive-quotes.html

Gaertner, Samuel and John Dovidio. "The Aversive Form of Racism," in *Prejudice, Discrimination and Racism*, edited by John Dovidio and Samuel Gaertner, 61-89. Cambridge, MA: Academic Press, Inc., 1986.

Giesen, Bernhard. "The Trauma of Perpetrators: The Holocaust as Traumatic Reference of German National Identity," in *Cultural Trauma and Collective Identity,* edited by Jeffrey C. Alexander, Ron Eyerman, Bernhard Giesen, Neil J. Smelser and Piotor Sztompka, 112-154. Berkley, CA: University of California Press, 2004.

Gramsci, Antonio. *Prison Notebooks, Volume II*, Trans. Joseph Buttigieg. New York: Columbia University Press, 1975.

Griffith, Janelle. "Man Sent Anti-Muslim Tweets to a Political Candidate Who Then Helped Pay His Medical Debt," *NBC News*, March 10, 2020. https://www.nbcnews.com/news/us -news/man-sent-anti-muslim-tweets-political-candidate-who-then-helped-n1154581.

Grohsgal, Dov and Kevin M. Kruse. "How the Republican Majority Emerged," *The Atlantic,* August 6, 2019. https://www.theatlantic.com/ideas/archive/2019/08/emerging -republican-majority/595504/

Grzanka, Patrick. "White Guilt: Race, Gender, Sexuality and Emergent Racism in the Contemporary United States," Ph.D. Diss. University of Maryland, College Park, 2020.

Hagedorn, Ann. *Beyond the River: The Untold Story of the Heroes of the Underground Railroad*. New York: Simon and Schuster, 2002.

Hammack, Philip. "Narrative and the Cultural Psychology of Identity," *Personal and Social Psychology Review*, 12 no. 3 (2008): 222-247.

Harper, Lisa Sharon. "The 'Little' White Lie That Has Divided Our Country," interviewed by Alex Gee, *Black Like Me*, July 3, 2018 Episode 21. http://blacklikeme.libsyn.com/lisa -sharon-harper-the-little-white-lie-that-has-divided-our-country

Harris, Cheryl. "Whiteness as Property," *Harvard Law Review*, 166 no. 8 (1993):1701-1791.

Harvey, Jennifer. *Dear White Christians: For Those Still Longing for Racial Reconciliation.* Grand Rapids, MI: William B. Eerdmans, 2014.

Heim, Joe. "Recounting of Rage, Violence and Death," *Washington Post,* August 14, 2017. https://www.washingtonpost.com/graphics/2017/local /charlottesville-timeline/

Helms, Janet. "Toward a Model of White Racial Identity Development" in *Black and White Racial Identity: Theory, Research and Practice,* edited by Janet Helms, 49-66. Westport, CT: Praeger Publishers, 1990.

Herzog, Frederick. "Black and White Together?" *Duke Divinity School Review*, 34 no. 2 (1969): 115-120.

Heschel, Abraham Joshua. "Religion and Race," in *Abraham Joshua Heschel: Essential Writings,* edited by Suzanna Heschel, 65-75. Maryknoll, NY: Orbis Books, 2011.

Hitchcock, Jeff. *Lifting the White Veil: An Exploration of White American Culture in a Multiracial Context*. Roselle, NJ: Crandie, Dostie & Douglass Books Inc., 2002.

Hill, Daniel. *White Awake: An Honest Look at What It Means to Be White*. Downers Grove, IL: InterVarsity Press, 2017.

History.com Editors. "The Homestead Act," *The History Channel*, April 24, 2020. https:// www.history.com/topics/american-civil-war/homestead-act

hooks, bell. *Yearning: Race, Gender and Cultural Politics*. Cambridge, MA: South End Press, 1990.

hooks, bell. "Representations of Whiteness in the Black Imagination," in *White Privilege: Essential Readings on the Other Side of Racism, Fifth Edition*, edited by Paul Rothenberg, 29-34. New York: MacMillan, 2016.

Horowitz, Juliana M., Anna Brown and Kiana Cox. "Race in America 2019," *Pew Research Center*, 2019. https://www.pewsocialtrends.org/2019/04/09/race-in-america-2019/

Howard, Gary. "White Man Dancing," in *Becoming and Unbecoming White: Owning and Disowning a Racial Identity,* edited by Christine Clark and James O'Donnell, 212-223. Westport, CT: Bergin and Garvey, 2019.

Howard, Gary. *We Can't Teach What We Don't Know: White Teachers, Multiracial Schools*. New York: Teachers College, 2006.

Hughes, Richard T. *Myths America Lives By: White Supremacy and the Stories That Give Us Meaning, Second Edition*. Champaign, IL: University of Illinois Press, 2018.

Hughey, Matthew. *The White Savior Film: Content, Critics, and Consumption*. Philadelphia: Temple University Press, 2014.

Hughey, Matthew. "Hegemonic Whiteness: From Structure and Agency to Identity Allegiance," in *The Construction of Whiteness*, edited by Stephen Middleton, David Roediger and Donald Shaffer, 212-223. Jackson, MS: University of Mississippi Press, 2016.

Hutchinson, Bill. "Deaths at Protests from Kenosha to Portland, but Motive Tells Different Story," *ABC News*, September 8, 2020. https://abcnews.go.com/US/deaths-connected-protests-story-complicated/story?id=72724790

Ignatiev, Noel. *How the Irish Became White*. New York: Routledge, 1995.

Isenberg, Nancy. *White Trash: The 400 Year Untold History of Class in America*. New York: Penguin Books, 2016.

Iyer, Aarti, Colin Wayne Leach and Faye Crosby. "White Guilt and Racial Compensation: The Benefits and Limits of Self-Focus," *Personality and Social Psychology Bulletin*, 29 no. 1, (2005): 117-129.

Jacobsen, Louis. "Michelle Obama Correct That the White House Was Built By Slaves," *Politifact*, July 25, 2016. https://www.politifact.com/factchecks/2016/jul/25/michelle-obama/michelle-obama-correct-white-house-was-built-slave/

Jensen, Robert. *The Heart of Whiteness: Confronting Race, Racism and White Privilege*. San Francisco: City Lights Books.

Johnson, Martenzie. "Joe McKnight and the Fear of the Black Man," *The UnDefeated*, December 5, 2016. https://theundefeated.com/features/joe-mcknight-and-the-fear-of-the-black-man/

Jones, James M. "The Color-Blind Racial Approach: Does Race Really Matter," in *The Myth of Racial Color Blindness: Manifestations, Dynamics and Impact,* edited by Helen A. Neville, Miguel Gallardo and Derald Wing Sue, 39-52. Washington, D.C.: American Psychological Association, 2019.

Jones, Solomon. "Facing Up to Racism of White Liberals," *Philadelphia Inquirer,* December 4, 2018. https://www.inquirer.com/columnists/yale-study-white-liberals-black -conversation-solomon-jones-20181204.html

Karimi, Faith. "Rachel Dolezal, White Woman Who Portrayed Herself as Black, Accused of Welfare Fraud," *CNN,* May 25, 2018. https://www.cnn.com/2018/05/25/us/rachel -dolezal-welfare-fraud-allegations/index.html

Kendi, Ibram X. *Stamped From the Beginning: The Definitive History of Racist Ideas in America.* New York: Nation Books, 2016.

Kendi, Ibram X. *How to Be an Antiracist.* New York: One World/Random House, 2019.

Kerr, Michael and Murray Bowen. *Family Evaluation: An Approach Based on Bowen Theory.* New York: W.W. Norton & Company, 1988.

Kimmel, Michael. *Angry White Men: American Masculinity at the End of an Era.* New York: Perseus Book Group, 2017.

King Jr., Martin. "Letter from a Birmingham Jail, *Why We Can't Wait.* New York: Putnam Publishers, 1963: 64-84.

Kirylo, James and Drick Boyd. *Paulo Freire: His Faith, Spirituality and Theology.* Rotterdam, The Netherlands: Sense Publishing, 2017.

Kivel, Paul. *Uprooting Racism: How White People Can Work for Racial Justice.* Gabriola Island, BC, Canada: New Society Publishers, 2017.

Kyrsan, Maria and Sarah Moberg. "A Portrait of African American and White Racial Attitudes," *University of Illinois Institute of Government & Public Affairs,* September 9, 2016. https://igpa.uillinois.edu/report/portrait-african-american-and-white-racial-attitudes

Labaton, Stephen. "Denny's Restaurants to Pay $54 Million in Race Bias Suits," *New York Times,* May 25, 1994. https://www.nytimes.com/1994/05/25/us/denny-s-restaurants -to-pay-54-million-in-race-bias-suits.html

Lane, Alexander. "The Legend of Slaves Building Capitol Is Correct," *Politifact,* January 19, 2009. https://www.politifact.com/factchecks/2009/jan/19/nancy-pelosi/legend -slaves-building-capitol-correct/

Lawrence, Steven. Interview by Author, April 9, 2019, Philadelphia, PA.

Laws, Mike. "Why We Capitalize 'Black' (and Not 'White')," *Columbia Journalism Review,* June 16, 2020. https://www.cjr.org/analysis/capital-b-black-styleguide.php

de Leon-Hartshorn, Iris, Tobin Miller Shearer and Regina Shands-Stoltzfus. *Set Free: A Journey Toward Solidarity Against Racism.* Scottdale, PA: Herald Press, 2010.

Liptak, Adam and Michael Wines. "Strict North Carolina Voter ID Law Thwarted After Supreme Court Rejects Case," *New York Times,* May 15, 2017. https://www.nytimes .com/2017/05/15/ us/politics/voter-id-laws-supreme-court-north-carolina.html

Lopez, Ian Haney. *Dog Whistle Politics: How Coded Racial Appeals Have Reinvented Racism and Wrecked the Middle Class.* New York: Oxford University Press, 2014.

Mather, Victor. "A Timeline of Colin Kaepernick vs. the N.F.L.," *New York Times*, February 15, 2019. https://www.nytimes.com/2019/02/15/sports/nfl-colin-kaepernick-protests-timeline.html

Mattheus, Antje and Lorraine Marino. *White People Confronting Racism*. Antje Mattheus and Lorraine Marino, 2011.

McCarthy, Bill. "The Death of George Floyd: What You Need to Know," *Politifact*, May 29, 2020. Politifact.com/article/2020/may/29/death-george-floyd-what-you-need-know

Menakem, Reesma. *My Grandmother's Hands: Racialized Trauma and the Pathway to Mending Our Hearts and Bodies*. Las Vegas: Central Recovery Press, 2017.

Metzl, Jonathan. *Dying of Whiteness: How the Politics of Racial Resentment Is Killing America's Heartland*. New York: Basic Books, 2019.

Mervosh, Sarah. "How Much Wealthier Are White School Districts Than Nonwhite Ones? $23 Billion Report Says," *New York Times*, February 27, 2019. https://www.nytimes.com / 2019/02/27/education/school-districts-funding-white-minorities.html?module=inline

Milloy, Courtland. "How American Oligarchs Created the Concept of Race to Divide and Conquer the Poor," *Washington Post*, April 9, 2016. https://www.washingtonpost.com /local/how-wealthy-americans-divided-and-conquered-the-poor-to-create-the-concept-of-race/2016/04/19/2cab6e38-0643-11e6-b283-e79d81c63c1b_story.html

Morriseau, Dominique. *Mud Row* (a play). Performed at the People's Light Theater, Malvern, PA, July 24, 2019.

Mueller, Jennifer. "Producing Colorblindness: Everyday Mechanisms of White Ignorance," *Social Problems*, 64 no. 2 (2017): 219-238.

National Public Radio. "Stories on Racial Disparities." https://www.npr.org/tags/ 371446041/ racial-disparities.

Norton, Michael I. and Samuel Sommers. "Whites See Racism As a Zero-Sum Game That They Are Now Losing," *Perspectives on Psychological Science*, 6 no. 3 (2011): 215-218.

Obama, Barack. "A More Perfect Union," delivered at the National Constitution Center, Philadelphia, PA, March 18, 2008. https://www.nytimes.com/2008/03/18 /us/politics/ 18text-obama.html

Obama, Michelle. "Transcript: Read Michelle Obama's full speech from the 2016 DNC," *CNN*, July 26, 2016. https://www.cnn.com/2016/07/26/politics/transcript-michelle -obama-speech-democratic-national-convention/index.html

Omi, Michael and Howard Winant. *Racial Formation in the United States, Third Edition*. New York: Routledge Press, 2015.

Padgett, Megan. "The Rise of the New White Nationalism in America," *University of Washington Digital Commons*, March 10, 2019. https://digitalcommons.tacoma.uw.edu/ history_thesis/37

Palmer, Parker. *A Hidden Wholeness: The Journey Toward the Undivided Life*. San Francisco: Jossey-Bass, 2004.

Pauls, Elizabeth Prine. "Native American History," *Encyclopedia Britannica* (no date). Accessed March 20, 2020 at https://www.britannica.com/topic/Native-American/Native-American-history

Peck, M. Scott. *The Road Less Traveled: A New Psychology of Love, Traditional Values and Spiritual Growth.* New York: Simon and Schuster, 1978.

Picca, Leslie H. and Joe R. Feagin. *Two-Faced Racism: Whites in the Backstage and Frontstage.* New York: Taylor and Francis, 2007.

Rice, James Douglas. "Bacon's Rebellion (1676-1677)," *Encyclopedia Virginia* (no date). https://www.encyclopediavirginia.org /bacon_s_rebellion_1676-1677

Roediger, David. *The Wages of Whiteness: Race and the Making of the American Working Class, Revised Edition.* New York: Verso, 2007.

Roithmayr, Daria. *Reproducing Racism: How Everyday Choices Lock in White Advantage.* New York: New York University Press, 2014.

Rooks, Noliwe. *Cutting School: Privatization and the End of Public Education.* New York: The New Press, 2017.

Saad, Layla F. *Me and White Supremacy: Combat Racism, Change the World and Become a Good Ancestor.* Naperville, IL: Source Books, 2020.

Shapiro, Ben. "The Myth of White Privilege." Speech delivered at the University of Missouri, Feb 26, 2017. https://www.youtube.com/watch?v=VO6nOocD1yg

Shor, Ira and Paulo Freire. A *Pedagogy for Liberation: Dialogues on Transforming Education.* Westport, CT: Bergin and Garvey, 1987.

Simba, Malik. "The Three-Fifths Clause of the United States Constitution (1787)," *Black Past*, October 3, 2014. https://www.blackpast.org/african-american-history/three-fifths-clause-united-states-constitution-1787/

Smedley, Audrey. *Race in North America: Origin and Evolution of a Worldview, Third Edition.* Boulder, CO: Westview Press, 2007.

Smith, Colin Bridges. "Telling Stories: Past and Present Heroes," *Frontiers: The Interdisciplinary Journal of Study Abroad*, 14 no. 1 (2007): 29-40.

Southern Poverty Law Center. *Speak Up: Responding to Everyday Bigotry.* Montgomery, AL: Southern Poverty Law Center, 2015. https://www.splcenter.org/20150125/speak-responding-everyday-bigotry

Southern Poverty Law Center. "White Nationalist" (no date).

https://www.splcenter.org/ fighting-hate/extremist-files/ideology/white-nationalist

Srivastava, Sarita. "Tears, Fears and Careers: Anti-Racism and Emotion in Social Movement Organizations," *Canadian Journal of Sociology*, 31 no. 1 (2006): 55-90.

Stapleford, John. "The Tortuous Journey: The Condition of Black America," *The Christian Scholars Review*, 37 no. 2 (2008): 231-251.

Steele, Shelby. *White Guilt: How Blacks and Whites Together Destroyed the Promise of the Civil Rights Era*. New York: Harper/Perennial, 2006.

Stempel, Jonathan. "PepsiCo Settles U.S. Charge of Racial Bias in Hiring," *Reuters*, January 11, 2012. https://www.reuters.com/article/us-pepsico-bias-settlement/pepsico-settles -u-s-charge-of-racial-bias-in-hiring-idUSTRE80A2A720120111

Stevenson, Howard. *Promoting Racial Literacy in Schools: Differences That Make a Difference*. New York: Teachers College Press, 2014.

Sue, Derald Wing, Christine Capodilupo, Gina Torino, Jennifer Bucceri, Aisha Holder, Kevin Nadal and Marta Esquilin. "Racial Microaggressions in Everyday Life: Implications for Clinical Practice," *American Psychologist*, 62 no. 4 (2007): 271-286.

Sue, Derald Wing. *Microaggressions in Everyday Life: Race, Gender and Sexual Orientation*. Hoboken, NJ: John Wiley & Sons, 2010.

Sue, Derald Wing. "Microaggressions: More Than Just Race," *Psychology Today*, November 17, 2010. https://www.psychologytoday.com/us/ blog/ microaggressions-in-everyday-life/201011/microaggressions-more-just-race

Sullivan, Shannon. *Good White People: The Problem with Middle Class White Anti-Racism*. Albany, NY: SUNY Press, 2014.

Tanner, Samuel Jaye. "Whiteness is a White Problem," *English Education,* 51 no. 2 (2019): 182-198.

Takaki, Ronald. *A Different Mirror: A History of Multicultural America, Revised Edition*. New York: Back Bay Books, 2008.

Tarca, Katherine. "Colorblind in Control: The Risks of Resisting Differences Amid Demographic Change," *Educational Studies*, 38 no. 2 (2015): 99-120.

Tatum, Beverly. *Why Are All the Black Kids Sitting Together in the Cafeteria? And Other Conversations About Race*. New York: Perseus Books, 1997.

Thandeka. *Learning to be White: Money, Race and God in America*. New York: Continuum/ Bloomsbury Academic, 2000.

Thomas, Nancy. "Study Finds Racial and Ethnic Disparities in Covid-19 Hospitalizations," *CNN,* August 17, 2020. https://www.cnn.com/2020/08/17/health/covid-19 -hospitalizations-racial-ethnic-disparities-study/index.html

Thompson, Becky and Veronica T. Watson. "Theorizing White Racial Trauma and Its Remedies," in *The Construction of Whiteness: An Interdisciplinary Analysis of Race Formation and the Meaning of White Identity*, edited by Stephen Middleton, David Roediger and Donald Shaffer, 234-255. Jackson, MS: University of Mississippi, 2016.

Thompson, Debra. "An Exoneration of Black Rage," *The South Atlantic Quarterly*, 116 no. 3 (2017): 457-481.

Tillman, James. *Why America Needs Racism and Poverty*. Atlanta, GA: James and Mary Tillman, 1969.

Unander, David. *Shattering the Myth of Race: Genetic Realities and Biblical Truths.* Valley Forge, PA: Judson Press, 2000.

U.S. Department of Justice. *Department of Justice Report Regarding the Criminal Investigation into the Shooting of Michael Brown by Ferguson Missouri Police Officer Darren Wilson,* March 4, 2015. https://www.justice.gov/sites/default/files/opa/press-releases/ attachments/2015/03/04/ doj_report_on_shooting_of_michael_brown_1.pdf

Victor, Daniel. "Bill O'Reilly Defends Comments About 'Well Fed' Slaves," *New York Times,* July 27, 2016. https://www.nytimes.com/ 2016/07/28/business/media/bill-oreilly-says-slaves-who-helped-build-white-house-were-well-fed.html

Villanueva, Edgar. *Decolonizing Wealth: Indigenous Wisdom to Heal the Divides and Restore Balance.* Oakland, CA: Berrett-Koehler, 2018.

Walsh, James D. "This Is America: Eleven Years After Obama's Election and Three Years into the Trump Presidency, the Threat of Domestic Terrorism Can't Be Ignored," *New York Magazine,* December 19, 2019. https://nymag.com/intelligencer/2019/12/white -supremacy-terrorism-in-america-2019.html

Warren, Mark. *Fire in the Heart: How White Activists Embrace Racial Justice.* New York: Oxford University Press, 2020.

Wildman, Stephanie. "The Persistence of White Privilege," *Washington University Journal of Law & Policy,* 18 (2005): 245-265. https://openscholarship.wustl.edu/cgi/ viewcontent.cgi /article=1262&context=law_journal_law_policy

Wise, Tim. *White Like Me: Reflections on Race from a Privileged Son.* Berkeley, CA: Soft Skull Press, 2011.

Wise, Tim. *Dear White America: Letter to a New Minority.* San Francisco: City Lights Books, 2012.

Wise, Tim. Author interview November 13, 2013.

White, Gillian B. "The Data Are Damning: How Race Influences School Funding," *The Atlantic,* Sept 30, 2015. http://www.theatlantic.com/business/archive/2015/09/ publicschoolfundingandtheroleofrace/408085/

Zhou, Li. "Trump's Racist References to the Coronavirus Are His Latest Effort to Stoke Xenophobia," *Vox,* June 23, 2020. https://www.vox.com/2020/6/23/21300332/trump -coronavirus-racism-asian-americans

Made in the USA
Las Vegas, NV
04 June 2021

24176675R00120